"This book is the best introduction I know to organized crime—what it is and how it operates, how it gains strength from globalization, and what law enforcement tools work best to defeat it."
— *Jack Goldsmith, Henry L. Shattuck Professor of Law at Harvard University, Former Assistant Attorney General, Head of the U.S. Justice Department's Office of Legal Counsel and Author of* The Terror Presidency: Law and Judgment Inside the Bush Administration.

"Phil and Steve Heymann's book on organized crime is a 'must read' for law enforcement practitioners. They describe the evolution of tactics, law, and strategy over the years to address the challenges of transnational organized crime."
— *Paul Evans, Former Police Commissioner of the Boston Police Department and Former Director of the Police Standards Unit of Britain's Home Office.*

"This book provides an analysis of the changing contest between organized crime and nation states. It persuasively presents the ideas we need today to deal with the danger of an alliance among terrorists, organized crime groups, supportive states, and private companies."
— *Luis Moreno Ocampo, First Chief Prosecutor of the International Criminal Court, Argentine Prosecutor in the "Trial of the Juntas."*

"Building on the extensive real world experience of the authors, this book is a whodunit for those concerned with how organized crime has operated and how law enforcement can meet it head on in this more international and high tech world."
— *Donald Stern, Former United States Attorney for the District of Massachusetts and Former Chair of the U.S. Attorney General's Advisory Committee.*

"If you want both the reality of organized crime and lucid analysis of its roots and methods of operation, these authors have written what you need."
— *Michael DeFeo, Former U.S. Justice Department Senior Counsel for International Law Enforcement in Rome, Former Assistant Director of the FBI and Former Deputy Chief of the U.S. Justice Department's Organized Crime and Racketeering Section.*

CHALLENGING ORGANIZED CRIME IN THE WESTERN HEMISPHERE

Challenging Organized Crime in the Western Hemisphere: A Game of Moves and Countermoves takes the unusual approach of exploring and describing how organized crime groups develop their capacities in response to heightened powers of law enforcement; and how law enforcement in turn responds, creating an ongoing dynamic interaction. The book shows how a state, such as the United States, has and can develop new laws and practices in ways that enable it to deal with relatively large violent groups—and yet preserve the rule of law and civil liberties.

While most texts approach organized crime groups and the challenges to government they impose from a static perspective, the authors dissect the interaction over time of organized crime and democratic governance that has created the present structure and balance of advantages in the United States. Readers learn about the markets for contraband and extortionate protection that form the bulk of organized criminal enterprise, the vulnerabilities of the traditional practices and rules of law enforcement, the effects of globalization of criminal enterprises on their contest with the state, the effectiveness of various practices of law enforcement, and the continuing forces of change, often technological, in the businesses of organized crime and law enforcement that play important roles in the contest between them.

This thought-provoking book is ideal for students of organized and transnational crime in university programs and law schools, as well as researchers and legal practitioners, who seek to look beyond the simple traditional history of organized crime and develop a strategy to confront organized crime in the future.

Philip Benjamin Heymann is the James Barr Ames Professor of Law Emeritus at the Harvard Law School. After graduation from Harvard Law School he clerked for U.S. Supreme Court Justice John Marshall Harlan. At the U.S. Department of Justice, he was then Assistant to the Solicitor General (1961–1965), Assistant U.S. Attorney General in charge of the Criminal Division (1978–1981) and Deputy Attorney General (1993–1994). At the U.S. Department of State (1965–1969), he was Acting Administrator of the Bureau of Security and Consular Affairs, Deputy Assistant Secretary of State for the Bureau of International Organizations and Executive Assistant to the Undersecretary of State.

Among the number of articles and books he has written while teaching at Harvard Law School, Heymann is the author of four books on combating terrorism: *Terrorism and America* (MIT Press 2000); *Terrorism, Freedom, and Security* (MIT Press 2003); *Protecting Liberty in an Age of Terror* with co-author Juliette Kayyem (MIT Press 2005); *Laws, Outlaws, and Terrorists* with co-author Gabriella Blum (MIT Press 2010). He is also the author of the *Politics of Public Management* (Yale University 1987) and *Living the Policy Process* (Oxford University Press 2008).

Stephen Philip Heymann's career as a federal prosecutor spanned over 32 years. During that time, he received commendations for his work from the Director of the FBI, the General Counsel for the Navy, the Director of the Secret Service and the Director of the Executive Office of U.S. Attorneys. He is the recipient of the Attorney General's Distinguished Service Award.

During his career, Stephen Heymann was a member of the Justice Department's elite Organized Crime Strike Force; established and directed one of the country's first, dedicated cybercrime units; and was Deputy Chief of the Criminal Division of the U.S. Attorney's Office in Boston, where he advised on all aspects of investigation and case structuring. Among his significant cases, he led what the FBI then described as one of the most significant Asian Organized Crime cases in its war against non-traditional organized crime; conducted the first court-authorized wiretap of a computer network, resulting in identification and charging of a foreign national breaking into U.S. military systems from Argentina; and successfully investigated a transnational group engaged in stealing tens of millions of credit and debit cards from TJX and other major U.S. retailers. The last was described by the Attorney General of the United States as the largest and most complex identity theft case then brought in the country.

CHALLENGING ORGANIZED CRIME IN THE WESTERN HEMISPHERE

A Game of Moves and Countermoves

Philip B. Heymann and Stephen P. Heymann

NEW YORK AND LONDON

First published 2019
by Routledge
711 Third Avenue, New York, NY 10017

and by Routledge
2 Park Square, Milton Park, Abingdon, Oxon, OX14 4RN

Routledge is an imprint of the Taylor & Francis Group, an informa business

© 2019 Taylor & Francis

The right of Philip B. Heymann and Stephen P. Heymann to be identified as authors
of this work has been asserted by them in accordance with sections 77 and 78 of the
Copyright, Designs and Patents Act 1988.

All rights reserved. No part of this book may be reprinted or reproduced or utilised
in any form or by any electronic, mechanical, or other means, now known or
hereafter invented, including photocopying and recording, or in any information
storage or retrieval system, without permission in writing from the publishers.

Trademark notice: Product or corporate names may be trademarks or registered trademarks,
and are used only for identification and explanation without intent to infringe.

Library of Congress Cataloging-in-Publication Data
Names: Heymann, Philip B., author. | Heymann, Stephen P., author.
Title: Challenging organized crime in the Western hemisphere : a game of
moves and countermoves / Philip B. Heymann and Stephen P. Heymann.
Description: New York, NY : Routledge, 2018. |
Includes bibliographical references and index.
Identifiers: LCCN 2018007360 (print) | LCCN 2018008004 (ebook) |
ISBN 9780429488313 (master) | ISBN 9781138595354 (hardback) |
ISBN 9781138595361 (pbk.)
Subjects: LCSH: Organized crime. | Transnational crime.
Classification: LCC HV6441 (ebook) | LCC HV6441 .H49 2018 (print) |
DDC 364.106–dc23
LC record available at https://lccn.loc.gov/2018007360

ISBN: 978-1-138-59535-4 (hbk)
ISBN: 978-1-138-59536-1 (pbk)
ISBN: 978-0-429-48831-3 (ebk)

Typeset Bembo
by Out of House Publishing

Latin America, which boasts just 8% of the world's population, accounts for 38% of its criminal killing. The butcher's bill in the region came to around 140,000 people last year, more than have been lost in wars around the world in almost all of the years this century.

— "Briefing Murder in Latin America: Shining some light," *The Economist*, April 7, 2018, republished with permission conveyed through Copyright Clearance Center, Inc.

CONTENTS

Prologue	*xi*
Acknowledgments	*xv*

PART ONE
The Business of Organized Crime (OC): The Concerns of States   **1**

1	What is Organized Crime?	5
2	The Sinaloa Cartel as a Concrete Example	7
3	Strategies for a State Addressing Organized Crime	17
4	A Final Issue of State Strategy: Rules of War or Law Enforcement	24
5	Detecting Visible Indications of Organized Crime	30

PART TWO
Law Enforcement on Steroids   **37**

6	The Mechanisms and Difficulties of Traditional Law Enforcement in Addressing Organized Crime	39
7	Creating a Law Enforcement Capacity to Address the Advantages of Organized Crime	43

x Contents

8 New Strategies for Prosecutors of Organized Crime 48

9 A Double-Edged Sword: How Improved Law Enforcement Aided Whitey Bulger 56

PART THREE
Globalization 71

10 Going International 73

11 International Law Enforcement Cooperation Pursuant to Treaties 77

12 The Colombian Connection: A Truly Cooperative Solution for an International Problem 81

13 Two Critical Ingredients of International Cooperation 94

PART FOUR
Moving the Proceeds of Organized Crime in Secret 99

14 Moving Proceeds of Crime without Revealing Their History 101

15 The Limited Effectiveness of a Barrage of Prohibitions of Money Laundering 108

PART FIVE
The Future of Organized Crime 113

16 The Internet and the Exploitation of the "Fog of War" 115

17 Conclusion: Predicting the Future of the Contest Between Nations and Sizable Criminal Enterprises 121

Bibliography *125*
Index *127*

PROLOGUE

It may seem to some that organized crime was a problem of the 20th century, now replaced in dangerousness and displaced in public concern by the 21st century forms of terrorism. That is *not* the view of American intelligence agencies or their leaders.

In February 2017, President Trump promulgated one of his earliest executive orders noting that: "Transnational criminal organizations ... have spread throughout the Nation, threatening the safety of the United States and its citizens." "A comprehensive and decisive approach is required to ... restore safety for the American people." To accomplish this, he placed the shared responsibilities on four cabinet level officials: the Secretary of State, the Attorney General, the Secretary of Homeland Security, and the Director of National Intelligence.

In May 2017, Director of National Intelligence Daniel Coates testified that Transnational Organized Crime was one of the top global threats to U.S. national security. In October, the National Drug Threat Assessment by the U.S. Drug Enforcement Administration reflected that Mexican transnational organized crime groups "remain the greatest criminal drug threat to the United States." Further, "illicit fentanyl and other synthetic opioids primarily sourced from China and Mexico" were contributing factors in a synthetic opioid epidemic causing a record number of deaths.

These are not U.S.-centric concerns. Violence in Mexico by the splintered remains of massive cartels has reached new heights. The United Nations Office on Drugs and Crime noted that in 2017 Europol identified 5,000 international organized crime groups operating in the European Union and widening their portfolios of illicit activities. The activities include not only drug trafficking and extortion but also arms trafficking, human trafficking, and a rich array of cybercrime. By 2017, 45 percent of all organized crime groups and 65 percent of drug trafficking groups were involved in more than one crime area. The U.N. office observes that the extent of this competition had put an emphasis on seeking new technologies and new strategies for new markets. In fact, new technologies and strategies have become abundant both for organized crime groups and for law enforcement.

It is not just the snapshot of organized crime in the world that causes fears. In the battle between organized crime and law enforcement, changes in technology, sociology, popular tastes and much more determine the relative likelihood of one or the other party pushing ahead of its rival. In this realm, much has been changing recently that favors organized crime in its battle with law enforcement.

There are new products created by changes in the world in the field of things that cannot legally be sold. Drugs have been joined by extensive human trafficking, often in the products of refugee crises throughout the world. Wars have added weapons sales to this market in contraband. New forms of extortion have become possible with attacks on electronically integrated networks.

Even within older product lines the changes are massive. New drugs and far more dangerous drugs such as fentanyl have replaced cocaine. These are highly concentrated and can be manufactured anywhere; they need not be grown and transported from fields historically targeted by drug enforcement agents. And a huge new market is rapidly developing openly in marijuana, potentially reducing its premium as contraband. As the product has shifted, so has the primary customer base which groups are targeting. The markets for drugs are changing as they shift from the older products once retailed by African American youths to opioids with their draw on rural areas and white populations. A high percentage of those becoming addicted to heroin started with opioids.

The sources for newly popular opioids are often in new areas of the world. For fentanyl, China competes with Mexico, increasing the number and dispersion of allies of organized crime. In the case of opioids, sales are also taking place through relatively open and massive diversion from pharmaceutical channels in the name of free access to painkiller prescriptions. The competition in the drug market now includes multinational companies operating openly and legally such as McKesson and Purdue Pharma.

Extortion, once generally a one-to-one threat by a thug, is no longer either. Ransomware sent out to infect victim computers over the Internet now enables criminal groups to threaten millions of people simultaneously, all without any physical presence. Cooperation can be managed across great distances in, for example, the sale of stolen personal identification. There are suddenly huge collections of customer data which can be stolen and used with the techniques of "big data."

Increasingly ubiquitous changes in computing and networking technology meanwhile are threatening the effectiveness of tools used by law enforcement to counter organized crime in recent years. As Europol's 2017 Internet Organized Crime Assessment underscores, while the "growing use of encryption is a boon to cybersecurity in general, its increasing use by the criminal community renders many traditional investigative techniques ineffective." "The use of encryption effectively and indefinitely [can] hide critical evidence," both communications between accomplices and records of their illicit activities.

Virtual currencies, such as Bitcoin, hamper law enforcement's ability to "follow the money" to critical actors. An organization's criminal infrastructure can now be far more fluid, and spread across multiple countries' jurisdictions, making it increasingly difficult for law enforcement in a single country to collect the evidence necessary to bring down the organization, or can often make unclear even what legal framework(s) regulate the collection of evidence or the crimes being committed.

Governments also may have some new advantages, such as in the ability to use the revealing records contained in the vast and diverse data routinely collected by legitimate businesses to put together a picture of organized crime and to identify its associates. However, on the whole, new technologies, new products, new areas of the world to work from, and broader cooperation favors organized crime.

In order to successfully address these new challenges, today's law enforcement officers and prosecutors must understand the tools, techniques and strategies which have been brought to bear, successfully and unsuccessfully, on organized crime groups over time. Only by understanding the constant give and take between the state and organized crime, their constant mutual adaptation, can future law enforcement officers and prosecutors develop the insights necessary to address the evolving forms and strategies of transnational organized crime groups affecting us today.

For more than a century the world has seen a contest of moves and countermoves between well-organized criminal enterprises and states demanding respect for their authority. But the contest has not been, like a tug-of-war, relatively constant and unchanging until one side or the other wins. Instead, advantages have fluctuated between criminal enterprises and law enforcement.

Not only have the businesses of criminal enterprises changed but broad strategies of each side have also changed, bringing about major shifts of power or advantage favoring states or, alternatively, large criminal organizations. This book illustrates and explains three such shifts: institutional and structural changes favoring law enforcement; globalization, creating a new balance between organized crime and law enforcement and state power; and technological changes favoring now one side and then the other.

Part One begins by describing the markets for contraband and "extortionate protection." The economic opportunities made available particularly by these markets induce and support sizable criminal enterprises. The shape of the enterprises is largely determined by the effort to meet two threats: the threat of law enforcement or military attacks; and the threat posed by rival criminal organizations.

Part Two describes the limited capacities and the substantial vulnerabilities of the traditional practices and rules of law enforcement, which were designed to punish and thus deter the crimes of a burglar, or robber, or a cheat—not to control a sizable well-armed and organized group of often ruthless criminals with the advantages of division of labor, experts, and often the sympathies of much of the public. To all this one should add that the corruptibility of law enforcement serves as a frightening "fifth column" in any contest between government and criminal businesses.

A criminal law that lacks both authority and power must either reorganize itself to attain both or shift its enforcement responsibilities to the often more trusted, and always more powerful, military. This is a shift that comes with a costly loss of civilian authority, civil liberties, and often political allegiance.

The United States adopted the alternative of reorganizing and, as Part Two explains, was the first nation to undertake major institutional changes in law enforcement to render the institutions and powers of criminal law—not just the military—capable of dealing with organized crime. The aptness of the U.S. diagnosis of its failings as late as the 1960s and the success of the remedies make it an important model for any nation aware of the need for, and potential power of, criminal law institutions. Part Two thus starts with a more precise depiction of the need for institutional change in dealing with organized crime and continues with a more precise account of the legislative, administrative, and investigatory nature of the changes that were made successfully in the United States.

More subtly, the new structures also required a change in prosecutorial and investigative roles and relationships. The new roles, relationships, and structures worked and the effectiveness of the institutions of U.S. law enforcement caught up with the capacities of sizable criminal enterprises. But, as we shall see, this required favorable background conditions as well as new and intelligent arrangements.

Part Three introduces the effects of globalization of criminal enterprises on their contest with the state—on the whole favoring organized crime. A criminal enterprise could protect itself by exploiting each nation's proud demand to control its own law enforcement within its own borders. The law enforcement of a single nation under attack by organized crime often found itself stymied by situations where the multinational locations of a criminal enterprise required the cooperation of several nations' law enforcement forces. Since investigation by one country in one or more other states without the other states' consent is forbidden by customary international law, the only equalizers for law enforcement

xiv Prologue

were treaties of cooperation in gathering evidence or in making a suspect available for trial. Neither worked well.

The only answer that works is to slowly build a level of trusting cooperation between two or more nations' police forces and between their prosecuting authorities—a relationship so trusting and so sharing in its antagonism to organized crime that the states freely waive their claims to exclusive control of law enforcement. This form of waiver allows a far stronger case to be built than either could or would alone. This proved to be a difficult goal with success a rare event even as globalization made transnational organized crime common.

Part Four explores the implication of the fact that law enforcement to disrupt the half-circle that represents smuggling contraband, such as drugs, into a country for sale should be, but is not generally, complemented by solid enforcement of the money laundering statutes that prohibit the other half-circle: moving cash proceeds from drug sales back across boundaries to other countries housing the growers, processors, transporters, smugglers, executives, and soldiers of the drug-selling cartel. The proceeds are hidden in a torrent of legitimate banking, investment, and commercial business, making it very difficult for law enforcement to seize cash proceeds or punish those moving them along the "return" half of the 360° cycle that is required to profit from a transnational business in contraband.

Finally, in Part Five we look at the continuing forces of change, often technological, in the businesses and practices of organized crime and law enforcement—changes that have occurred and those that we can only see if we squint into the fog-covered future. The use of the Internet by organized crime is a change that has already occurred, enabling more unified management of an organization's remote projects and new forms of fraud and extortion.

It is as important to say what the book is not as it is to describe its coverage. The book does not join the articles and books carefully relating the structure, methods, and criminal products of an array of organized crime enterprises in scores of countries. Our method is different. Our general arguments are based on clarifying ideas about the problems of carrying out illegal businesses in a context of challenges by law enforcement and rival gangs. We support the general arguments by detailed illustrations of particular criminal enterprises facing competitive rivalries and law enforcement agencies.

The bibliography includes dozens of additional illustrations of how particular organized crime enterprises have worked. But they remain illustrations, not hard data, held together by recognizing the common challenges that must be addressed by groups seeking to exploit opportunities for profit in a dangerously lawless part of the overall market.

This methodology also explains the absence of footnotes except to provide the sources for the factual accounts of specific criminal enterprises and of law enforcement cooperation between states that we provide in the form of three case studies. This is an essay on the broadest common characteristics of organized criminal groups and their derivation from the environment in which they must function; we therefore haven't found other source notations essential or useful in a book the purpose of which is to demonstrate the "logic" of an ongoing struggle between organized crime and law enforcement. We have chosen not to use references to the writings of authorities to bolster the power of our arguments, although a number of the most useful authorities appear in the bibliography.

ACKNOWLEDGMENTS

The authors have been assisted by several groups of people in the production of this book. It is useful to state the contributions in a chronological order.

The starting point of the research on organized crime groups we needed was bibliographic research, of very high quality, provided again and again by Aslihan Bulut, Librarian for International, Foreign, and Comparative Law at Harvard Law School, using the vast resources of Harvard Law School's library. This produced files of studies of organized crime groups—studies that were supplemented in some cases by student and author interviews of individuals involved in the prosecution of the groups in the United States, Mexico, and Colombia.

Writing up the information in the files in informative as well as accurate drafts was the assignment of a half-dozen or more talented students who produced drafts of the illustrative accounts used to provide concrete examples of the authors' points. They worked under the editorship of Lisa Brem and the authors. We owe our thanks and admiration to the student researchers who worked on the following accounts: the first, Sinaloa, worked on by Amanda Liverzoni and Michael Soyfer; the second, The Case of Whitey Bulger, was researched by Georgia Stasinopoulosen; and the third, Money Laundering in Colombia, by Sean Driscoll. Other accounts include: the Juárez Cartel researched by Amanda Liverzoni; Albert Gonzales by Sharon Kim; Las Vedas by Sophie Elsne; and The Growth of Organized Crime in the United States by Alicia Corvetto, Ari Rubin, and Elizabeth Maroni. In one case the work provided by the student, Nicholas Maietta, involved not just history, but an analytic explanation of the complexities of money laundering and virtual currencies. For that work, Nicholas Maietta deserves special acknowledgment and our thanks. He made available to us an expertise that we needed as well as illustrative accounts of difficult financial aspects of organized crime.

The process of researching and writing this book was largely supervised by Lisa Brem, manager of the Teaching, Learning, and Curriculum Solutions Department in the Harvard Law School Library. Lisa worked enthusiastically and highly professionally over a period of several years: managing and editing student case researchers; revising their drafts; discussing the structure of the cases and manuscript with the authors; and commenting on the final drafts. We owe her a great deal for her remarkable skills, perseverance, and friendship.

xvi Acknowledgments

Lighter but still important hands in final editing were played by Ann Heymann and Cynthia LuBien, our wives, and by Margaret McDonald, a dear friend and a professional editor of countless reports and documents.

Keeping track of the work products as they moved to their final stages, typing the manuscript, and then typing the manuscript again, with good humor and great efficiency were the responsibilities of Sandra Mays, Professor Heymann's administrative assistant. There is much we could not have done without her. With that the role of others was complete, except for the extremely helpful and efficient work of the publishers. Building, organizing, illustrating and explaining the analytic structure of this book was the sole responsibility of the two authors from the beginning. This process shaped the structure and content of the book.

The views expressed in this book are those of the authors alone and do not necessarily represent the views of the United States Department of Justice or the U.S. Attorney's Office for the District of Massachusetts.

PART ONE

The Business of Organized Crime (OC)

The Concerns of States

Introduction

What is "organized crime"? The answer depends on whether it is to be defined by the fact that it involves the organization of several people engaged in crime; by the particular type of businesses the organization is very likely to be involved in; by its use of corruption and intimidation (i.e., by the special requirements of surviving in a lucrative illegal market); by the concerns it generates in states; or by the focus of a certain set of public fears.

The United Nations Convention Against Organized Crime defines an organized criminal group (an "OCG") as, "a structured group of three or more persons, existing for a period of time and acting in concert with the aim of committing one or more serious crimes … to obtain … a material benefit." The reference to "three or more persons" even when supplemented by "existing for a period of time" seems too minimal a danger to explain the need for a U.N. Convention or to capture the concerns that organized crime often raises in citizens and state officials. The reference to the members acting "in concert … to obtain … a material benefit" doesn't suggest a threat any more serious than other quite ordinary crimes—for example, those of a group of home burglars.

Organized crime's closest cousin in terms of governmental concern about nonstate dangers, and especially globalized private threats, is terrorism. Organized crime differs from terrorism in terms of the last words of the U.N. definition: the motivation for the organization and its activities must be "a material benefit" in the case of organized crime as opposed to changed government policy in the case of terrorism. The U.N. definition reflects only the fears aroused by a group of criminals reaping the benefits of economies of scale and division of labor while carrying on some kind of "serious" illegal business over time. That is very close to the thousands of quite ordinary conspiracies prosecuted each year in a jurisdiction following the common law.

There have been serious efforts to define the primary businesses of organized crime. The leading contenders are the sale of contraband (particularly drugs) and extortion of payments by threats (often described as "for protection") from illegitimate and legitimate businesses. Gambling and loan-sharking

2 Part I

would once have been prominent in the contraband categories—until those businesses developed strong legal competition.

The businesses reflect the market niche of organized crime in the vastly larger market of a modern nation. The niche in the case of the sale of contraband is plainly the absence of legitimate competition in meeting a consumer demand—competition to which a legal business would have to adjust if selling automobiles or toothpaste. There is a strong market for the contraband. It can be manufactured, grown, or purchased at a low price, and then processed, transported, and sold at a price many times as high without legal competition to drive the price down.

The other noteworthy business is extortion of small illegal businesses which cannot turn to government for protection without risk of being themselves prosecuted; or extortion of legal businesses (like international shipping, the disposal of garbage, or the renting of equipment to restaurants) which can be deterred by the organization's threats (or by feeble state law enforcement capacity) from calling on law enforcement for protection. Labor racketeering to threaten businesses falls into this category. Once again the illegality of extortion—combined with the power to intimidate the victim into silence or the impunity that comes with secrecy in carrying out the threat in a way and at a time of the OCG's choosing—creates a niche where legal businesses cannot compete and from which illegal rivals can be pushed by fear of armed attacks.

Organized crime could, alternatively, be defined by its reliance on corruption to enable its customers and suppliers, as well as itself, to avoid the risks of law enforcement; and by its use of intimidation to disrupt the orderly but dangerous legal passage from a complaint to the police, through an investigation, to an arrest and charge, and then on to the presentation of witnesses and a verdict.

Organized crime could be instead defined by its need to find alternative methods to simply carry on its business. That need comes with a set of special characteristics of working in a "market" where there is no enforcement of contracts, no government protection against fraud and theft, and no legal enforcement of the promises and other obligations that create business relationships. Much of the day-to-day operations of an organization selling contraband will look like the activities of an organization selling a perfectly legal commodity; but other parts of it will look very different and very challenging.

Organized crime might be defined by the ordinary citizen's fears of having to rely on his own means, without the government support that citizens have relied on for centuries, to prevent a private group from carrying out punishment for disobedience to its will, or to enable individuals to protect their own property, or to invest without fear of extortion. The fear of terrorism is different; it is felt by a public that senses the randomness of this danger and thus the impossibility of avoiding it. In contrast, public fear of organized crime is of its ability to enforce its will on individuals who cannot safely or effectively bring the often-far-greater force of the state to bear as protection. Indeed, in some cases organized crime may even be actively supported by the state, as it has been in Russia and Argentina.

Closely related, organized crime may be defined by the set of state concerns that motivate an ongoing governmental challenge to the criminal organization's very existence and to the well-being of its members. Those government concerns include: whatever motivated the creation of a contraband category for certain goods and services or for making extortion a serious crime. (Extortion of small-time crooks may not be a cause for major concern to governments, but extortion of legal businesses or private individuals by kidnapping family members more directly challenges the state's responsibility for the security of its citizens.) A government may be concerned to preserve a citizen's sense of safety in freely choosing his behavior when he is complying with the law, or it may fear the surprisingly regular and dangerous violence that almost always accompanies the business of organized crime. Finally, the government may fear the loss of trust in the state that comes with its penetration by criminals and the capture of important government institutions.

The National Security Council of the United States developed its own definition of transnational organized crime:

> The self-perpetuating association of individuals who operate transnationally for the purpose of attaining power, influence, monetary and/or commercial gains, wholly or in part, by illegal means while protecting their activities through a pattern of corruption and/or violence ... or the exploitation of transnational commerce or communication mechanisms.

The primary function of a definition of organized crime, when the activities are already criminal anyway, is to allow recognition of where efforts to deal with these concerns should be focused. For the NSC group, one of the categories of harm is far more compelling than the others. The gravest concern of a nation faced with organized crime is that support for state institutions and the trustworthy operations of government are undermined by the inability of citizens to trust the political levels of government, their inability to rely upon the vigor of law enforcement, and their inability to enjoy the sense of freedom that comes with the applicability of the law even to the strong, the rich, and the ruthless.

1

WHAT IS ORGANIZED CRIME?

Countering Organized Crime

Transnational organized crime is often on the list of the five to ten major threats to the national security of the United States. This book explores why it makes this list and how capable we are of defusing, if not defeating, that threat. Describing our efforts to defeat this threat requires first analyzing what are the primary money-making activities of organized crime, what capacities and steps to fend off law enforcement and rival organized crime groups (OCGs) are available to it, and what it is about these activities and capacities that is of real concern to a nation or an alliance of nations.

Each of these questions varies with the time and place of operations and with the strategies of the organization and of the government resisting it. Still, it helps to simplify the problem in a half-dozen ways.

1. The two primary profit-making activities of organized crime have been, for some time, trafficking in contraband goods or services and extortion of legitimate and illegitimate businesses. (The Internet may be adding a third: theft of identities and of intellectual property.)
2. As the U.S. National Security Council noted, to continue in business for some time, an organized crime group generally must use either corruption and intimidation of law enforcement or the advantage of working transnationally from a haven state.
3. To protect its market advantages an OCG must be able and willing to use violence against its rivals.
4. To move contraband from source countries (such as Colombia) to customers in another nation, such as the United States, and then to return the proceeds to Colombia an OC business must adjust to a recognizable set of problems that Starbucks doesn't face in the coffee business.
5. There is a familiar list of types of consequences a nation may fear from uncontrolled organized crime. Understanding the types helps define the remedies.
6. There are three ways a nation can develop the capacities needed to eliminate or control organized crime.
   a. By traditional law enforcement after corruption and intimidation are controlled; or, as in the case of the United States, by new and specially empowered forms of law enforcement.

6 Chapter 1

    b.   By the use of military and intelligence powers and rules of engagement, as was done in Colombia and, to a lesser extent, Mexico.

    c.   By forming alliances with rival OCGs or allied nations hostile to the group that law enforcement seeks to eliminate. (Whitey Bulger's Winter Hill OCG helped eliminate its Italian rivals in Boston; the Cali Cartel helped end Pablo Escobar's Medellin Cartel.)

Of course the organized crime groups can vary sharply in other aspects of their activities, capacities, and strategies, and the same is true of the nations combating them. And the community surrounding an OCG can be more or less supportive of the group. Still, these six broad variations will go far to explain how nations address organized crime.

2

THE SINALOA CARTEL AS A CONCRETE EXAMPLE

Introduction

In Part One we address the most basic and often unresolved questions about the very nature of organized crime: What are the special characteristics that make a cocaine-dealing "cartel" (like Sinaloa) different from both a large coffee business (like Starbucks) and from ordinary street or white-collar criminals? What are the difficulties or opportunities that exist only for organized crime and that bring about the special characteristics that distinguish it?

Part One also focuses on what it is about these special characteristics that are of great concern to governments; what options governments have to deal with those concerns; and how they choose between exploiting the options that come with using security forces (the military and intelligence) or using only familiar law enforcement power, or, as the U.S. has done, develop an intermediary possibility that is law enforcement with importantly enhanced powers.

Those are very general questions about what turns out to be a contest between a state with specific capacities and an organized crime group embedded in a very particular context that generates its own special set of needs and capacities. Both differences in state capacities and differences in the situation of the OCG makes dealing with the Sinaloa Cartel in Mexico very different from dealing with La Cosa Nostra in New York, Boryokudan in Japan or the Russian Mafia.

This book does not contain a compendium of organized crime groups worldwide. There are already several good examples that feature such a compendium, including notably *McMafia: A Journey Through the Global Criminal Underworld* by Misha Glenny. Rather, in each of the sections we will use case studies of organized crime groups and investigations of organized crime groups to provide richly textured examples of the points we are making.

Because we want to focus on dangers to the United States we will emphasize responses to threats from organized crime groups near to the United States when we address specific variations on the general problem of organized crime. In Part One our examples often involve Colombian and Mexican groups. Until early in 2016 the Sinaloa Cartel was the most successful of these; so we begin by providing a rather

8 Chapter 2

full description of its history, special capacities, choice of money-making activities, organization, handling of funds, and much more.

More than any other cartel, Sinaloa epitomizes a business operation. Conservative estimates placed the Sinaloa Cartel's annual revenue at upwards of $3 billion,[1] which, were it not an illegal enterprise, would have made it one of the forty largest companies in Mexico and a member of the Latin 500.[2] The figurative CEO of the organization was—and perhaps still is—Joaquín "El Chapo" Guzmán Loera. Born into rural poverty, Guzmán Loera constructed a vast empire out of marijuana, cocaine, heroin, and methamphetamine, the proceeds from which landed him on *Forbes* magazine's annual billionaires list from 2009 through 2012 (his absence from the 2013 list was due to their inability to reach Guzmán Loera to verify his assets).[3] Under his tenure, the Sinaloa Cartel burgeoned into a complex, multinational organization that, according to some estimates, controlled forty to sixty percent of drug trafficking into the United States and was expanding its operations across the globe.[4]

History of the Sinaloa Cartel

The Sinaloa Cartel is an offshoot of one of the oldest smuggling operations in Mexico. In the 1940s Mexican traffickers began cooperating with organized crime groups from the United States to move product across the border. This cooperation developed into large-scale drug trafficking organizations by the 1960s.[5] Pedro Avilés Pérez took advantage of this climate to build Mexico's first major drug cartel in the Mexican state of Sinaloa. Avilés Pérez's organization controlled much of the marijuana and heroin imported into the United States during the 1970s. He pioneered the strategic bribery and intimidation of public officials and the airplane transport of contraband—techniques that modern-day Mexican cartels still use. Like many drug traffickers, however, Avilés Pérez's career was short; it came to an end in 1978, when the Mexican federal police killed him during a shootout. Following Avilés Pérez's death, Miguel Ángel Félix Gallardo, a former federal police officer, took control of the organization.[6] Félix Gallardo soon controlled almost all of the Mexican drug trade and quickly moved to expand it further. With the Colombian cartels weakening throughout the 1980s, Félix Gallardo began to demand payment in product. The power structure shifted, and the Colombian cartels became mere suppliers to Félix Gallardo's Mexican organization.

The Guadalajara Cartel—as Félix Gallardo's organization came to be known during the 1980s— operated with impunity in its home bases. Law enforcement officials, either on the organization's payroll or fearing retribution, overlooked crimes committed by drug traffickers, even those unrelated to drug trafficking. In 1985, however, Félix Gallardo ordered the torture and execution of an undercover United States Drug Enforcement Administration (DEA) officer, Enrique Camarena, whose information had resulted in the discovery and dismantling of a large marijuana plantation. Camarena's murder triggered a powerful reaction from the United States government. United States pressure on Mexican authorities, along with the 1987 election of Miguel de la Madrid Hurtado, an anti-cartel president, brought an end to the Guadalajara Cartel. Mexican troops arrested Félix Gallardo in 1989, and the government moved him to a new maximum security prison in 1992 after discovering that he had continued to participate in cartel operations in prison with the help of a cell phone.[7]

As the United States and Mexico were zealously pursuing his cartel, Félix Gallardo decided to protect his empire by dividing it into several sub-cartels in 1987.[8] After his arrest, the Guadalajara Cartel split into four separate organizations, the Tijuana (Arellano Félix), Juárez (Carrillo Fuentes), Gulf, and Sinaloa Cartels. The modern-day Sinaloa Cartel was formed in 1988 by Guzmán Loera and Héctor Luis "El Güero" Palma Salazar. Guzmán Loera took full control of the cartel after Palma Salazar's arrest in 1995 (although Guzmán Loera was himself incarcerated at the time).[9]

Guzmán Loera was born in the small mountain town of La Tuna, where his father grew poppies. In the state in which La Tuna is situated, few jobs existed outside of the drug trade, which Guzmán Loera quickly joined. With only a third-grade education, he proved adept at coordinating drug trafficking into the United States and eventually became a top lieutenant to Félix Gallardo.[10]

Building the Sinaloa Cartel into Mexico's largest drug trafficking organization involved a great deal of hard work, brutality, and cunning. When Félix Gallardo distributed smuggling routes among the sub-cartels, Sinaloa received some of the worst routes. Initially, Sinaloa paid *piso* (tribute) in order to use the Tijuana Cartel's routes. Tijuana, though particularly violent, was among the weaker cartels. After Félix Gallardo's arrest, Sinaloa immediately began an aggressive expansion by targeting the Tijuana Cartel. Sinaloa allied with the Juárez Cartel in the ensuing conflict, which became spectacularly violent. Early in the conflict, the Tijuana Cartel beheaded Palma Salazar's wife and threw his two small children off of a bridge, possibly at the incarcerated Félix Gallardo's behest.[11] Later, Guzmán Loera arranged to assassinate the Arellano Félix brothers, the leaders of the Tijuana Cartel, while they were at a nightclub. Sinaloa's gunmen killed several people, but the Arellano Félix brothers survived by escaping through the bathroom window.[12]

The Arellano Félix brothers struck back at Sinaloa in 1993 by trying to assassinate Guzmán Loera as his car pulled up to the Guadalajara airport. Guzmán Loera escaped unharmed and, in a tragic mistake, the assassins instead killed Cardinal Juan Jesús Posadas Ocampo. The Cardinal's death proved too outrageous for the Mexican government to ignore, and Guzmán Loera was arrested in 1993. Despite his incarceration in a maximum security facility, Guzmán Loera continued to run the Sinaloa Cartel by using a cell phone. Having bribed or intimidated nearly everyone in the prison, including the warden, Guzmán Loera enjoyed significant perks in the facility, including conjugal visits and well-appointed, private rooms.[13] In 2001, believing that the incoming Fox administration would extradite him to the United States, Guzmán Loera spent $2.5 million bribing prison guards and law enforcement officials to facilitate his escape from prison. While he was concealed in a laundry basket, Guzmán Loera's associates simply rolled him out of prison.[14]

Structure and Operations of the Sinaloa Cartel

The contemporary Sinaloa Cartel is structured so that central operations mainly provide backward and forward linkages from cultivators and suppliers to wholesalers and dealers in the United States and elsewhere.[15] Sinaloa is itself a loose confederation of smaller regional organizations, all working together under the umbrella of Guzmán Loera's cartel. Senior figures within the Sinaloa Cartel tend to operate semi-autonomously, though they share smuggling infrastructure and coordinate closely with one another.[16] The most significant figures, after Guzmán Loera, were Ismael "El Mayo" Zambada García and Ignacio "Nacho" Coronel Villarreal, who was killed in 2010. The day-to-day management of the cartel rests largely with powerful regional plaza bosses responsible for coordinating smuggling and cartel operations within their territory. As of May 2013, the U.S. Department of Treasury's Office of Foreign Assets Control had identified eight such Sinaloa Cartel plaza bosses.[17]

10 Chapter 2

Business Lines

Outside of the central structure, Sinaloa relies largely on partnerships and contractors to obtain its products and ship them to users in the United States. The Sinaloa Cartel procures drugs like cocaine, marijuana, and opiates from a variety of rural farms and even some cartel-owned plantations throughout Latin America. Some evidence suggests that the cartel may also be growing marijuana within the United States on federal land.[18] After receiving the raw ingredients, the cartel then processes and packages these drugs for delivery across the border in the United States. Marijuana is among the cartel's largest producers of revenue, and the cartel often uses revenues from sales of marijuana to make expensive investments in other areas of its business. Cocaine is also a high-earner and has a high value-to-weight ratio, making it relatively easy and profitable for the cartel to smuggle. By contrast, heroin is more difficult and expensive to produce, but it is also easy to transport. Reportedly, Guzmán Loera took particular pride in the quality of Sinaloa's heroin.[19]

In recent years, Sinaloa has also become more involved in methamphetamine ("meth") production and trafficking. Some report that it was Coronel Villarreal who first recognized the revenue potential of methamphetamine,[20] while others report that Sinaloa's alliance with Guadalajara's Colima Cartel led it into the meth business.[21] Regardless, methamphetamine trafficking was a highly profitable innovation for the Sinaloa Cartel. While legislative responses to restrict the sale of precursor chemicals have made the drug more difficult to manufacture in the United States, production has continued in Mexico. Until his arrest in 2007, Zhenli Ye Gon, a Mexican-Chinese businessman, provided a connection between manufacturers of meth-precursor chemicals in Southeast Asia and the Sinaloa Cartel. Once it gained access to precursor chemicals, the cartel could produce the drug in its own illicit laboratories throughout Mexico and, to the extent possible, the United States.[22]

Some reports suggest that meth may have overtaken cocaine to become the world's second most-used drug after marijuana.[23] Sinaloa's expansion into meth production has been valuable to the cartel for a number of reasons. Since meth is artificially synthesized, it can be made almost entirely indoors out of otherwise legal ingredients through a process that does not rely on farmers. Because of this, Sinaloa has constructed "superlabs" to produce vast quantities of meth. Large seizures of precursor ingredients hint at the scale of Mexican meth production: the Mexican government seized an astonishing 252 tons of meth precursors at ports in December 2011 alone.[24] Like cocaine and heroin, meth is relatively easy to smuggle, and small amounts can reap a large profit. Meth is also extremely addictive. To capitalize on this quality, Sinaloa initially included "free samples" of meth in its shipments of other drugs to wholesalers in an attempt to enter the United States meth market. This tactic seems to have succeeded.[25]

Distribution

The Sinaloa Cartel possesses unparalleled expertise in smuggling their products across the border. An indictment filed against Guzmán Loera in the United States District Court for the Northern District of Illinois illustrates a variety of tactics employed by the cartel. Guzmán Loera and his associates are accused in the indictment of coordinating the transportation of drugs "using various means, including but not limited to, Boeing 747 cargo aircraft, private aircraft, submarines and other submersible and semi-submersible vessels, container ships, go-fast boats, fishing vessels, buses, rail cars, tractor trailers, and automobiles."[26]

Guzmán Loera has long been viewed as an innovator in moving his illicit products, often resorting to clever and surprising methods. Stories abound of drug shipments hidden in containers of cooking oil, rolls of chicken wire, and inside oil tankers.[27] In 1993, cans of jalapeno peppers bearing the label "La Comadre" and stuffed with over seven tons of Sinaloa cocaine were seized in Baja California. The cans were to be shipped to Los Angeles where Guzmán Loera had established a relationship with grocer and owner of Tia Anita foods Jose Reynosa Gonzalez.[28] The cartel is known to use boats and ships in the Pacific, but has also employed more sophisticated methods such as semi- and fully-submersible submarines.

In addition to all of these convoluted and large-scale trafficking methods, Sinaloa continues to rely on simple yet highly effective options: the cartel installs special cavities in the bodies of cars, hides drugs in truckloads of fish, sends small shipments across the border in otherwise inconspicuous cars, and even ships drugs through FedEx. Frequently, Sinaloa smugglers cross the border illegally. In one instance, the U.S. government constructed an expensive, high-tech fence in Arizona, only to discover that Sinaloa had, in the meantime, constructed a catapult capable of flinging several hundred pounds of marijuana over the fence.[29] These low-tech, small smuggling operations may not be the most efficient method of moving drugs across the border, but they help Sinaloa guard against large losses in the event of a law enforcement seizure. Guzmán Loera and his associates would sometimes even pool and split their shipments among smugglers in order to spread their risk more widely.[30]

Guzmán Loera was also a pioneer in the use of underground tunnels. The Sinaloa Cartel's tunnel systems are often complex and difficult to discover. Some tunnels even feature air conditioning and trolley lines to accommodate heavy shipments.[31] Equipment for digging tunnels can cost up to $75,000 and the final product may contain hydraulic lifts, elevators, and power generators.[32] Around 1990, Guzmán Loera commissioned Mexican architect Felipe de Jesus Corona to build the cartel's first major tunnel, a 200-foot-long concrete-lined passageway under the border from Tijuana to San Diego. Dubbed "Cocaine Alley," the tunnel was an impressive feat of engineering. The entrance to the tunnel lay under the home of cartel attorney Agua Prieta and was accessible only by turning on a faucet tap outside the house which would then trigger a secret hydraulic lift under a pool table inside.[33] Over the years the Sinaloa Cartel has continued to refine and extend their tunnel systems. Between 2006 and 2010, fifty-one tunnels were found in the city of Nogales alone,[34] almost of all of which were believed by the U.S. Immigration and Customs Enforcement agency (ICE) to be the handiwork of the Sinaloa Cartel.[35]

Once the drugs reach the United States, with the exception of a few large wholesalers, individuals involved in the drug distribution are typically only loosely connected to the Sinaloa Cartel. With the help of urban gangs, these individuals deliver the Sinaloa's product to drug users. Unlike in Mexico, where Guzmán Loera often establishes relationships with wholesale distributors and negotiates with them directly, wholesalers in the United States operate autonomously. Because few distributors have enough cash on hand to make upfront payments to the cartel, trusted wholesalers often buy drugs on credit and pay the cartel only after they sell the drugs. Some particularly valuable wholesalers even have the ability to negotiate prices down from the cartel's initial asking price.[36] Guzmán Loera demonstrated little interest in dismantling this vast and confusing web of middlemen and connecting the cartel directly to its American customers.

Money Laundering

Gaining access to revenue generated by the sale of drugs successfully smuggled into the United States is one of the most difficult parts of Sinaloa's business. Although risky, the cartel manages to move some of its money into banks. The difficulty of money laundering can be measured by the fee that the cartel must

12 Chapter 2

pay to its money launderers: a service fee of about fifteen cents on the dollar.[37] The U.S. government has had some success using the Foreign Narcotics Kingpin Designation Act to impose sanctions on major drug traffickers, which has curtailed the cartel's ability to infiltrate U.S. financial institutions.

Much of Sinaloa's money, however, remains in cash, and raids of cartel operatives' houses have resulted in massive cash seizures. Unseized money sneaks across the border into Mexico, where it gathers in the living rooms and safes of drug lords' houses. As mentioned previously, when Mexican authorities raided the house of Mexican-Chinese businessman Zhenli Ye Gon they discovered $206 million in cash.[38] Much of this is the cash left over after the cartel has paid its bribes, compensated its direct employees, and reinvested a sizable portion of its revenue back into its own operations.

Bribery

The money that goes toward bribing government officials and law enforcement is vital to the cartel's success. While Sinaloa may be able to avoid paying taxes, their bribes might rival the effective tax rate. Bribery was widespread during the PRI's long reign over Mexican politics. While the practice of bribery did not end after the PRI fell out of power in 2000, it did become somewhat more complex to execute. However, the benefits of bribery are profound: Sinaloa has been able to convince law enforcement officials to overlook its activities, penalize rivals, and return seized contraband through the use of bribes. In some cases, police officers have even acted as enforcers for the cartel (though Sinaloa's assassins also pose as police officers). The police are not the only targets of bribery. Cartel leaders have lived luxuriously and continued to run their cartels while incarcerated after bribing corrections officials. The cartel also bribes mayors, governors, and high-level officials. Noe Ramirez, President Felipe Calderón's drug czar, was charged with accepting $450,000 in bribes each month.[39]

Even with the added scrutiny of the cartel's leaders by U.S. law enforcement, most believe Sinaloa will continue to thrive. As Ismael "El Mayo" Zambada García, one of Sinaloa's highest ranking leaders, said in a rare interview: "When it comes to the capos, jailed, dead, or extradited, their replacements are ready."[40]

Another Great "El Chapo" Escape

After the 2001 prison escape from Puente Grande, near Guadalajara, Guzmán Loera maintained a low profile. He observed the Mexican authorities capture and kill "the leaders of every group that challenged his Sinaloa Cartel's spot at the top of global drug trafficking."[41] In January 2014, the noose was tightening, as federal forces killed one of the Sinaloa Cartel's main lieutenants and captured ten henchmen.[42] One month later, Guzmán Loera made the fatal misstep of coming out of hiding and venturing into the city of Culiacán to indulge in some of the sensual comforts the city had to offer.[43] The U.S. DEA was in close pursuit, and he fled south to the beach community of Mazatlán where he was then captured by the Mexican marines "without a shot being fired."[44] Guzmán Loera was sent to prison in Mexico while the U.S. and Mexican authorities wrestled with who had jurisdiction to try him first.

On July 11, 2015, 16 months after being captured, a well-executed escape plan was implemented at a Mexican super-maximum security prison, Altiplano. Within moments of entering his shower cell, the notorious Sinaloa Cartel boss slipped through a square 20-by-20-inch drain hole and into oblivion.[45]

Government officials and tunnel experts believe that Guzmán Loera's inner circle enlisted the services of an architect, a contractor, a tunnel project manager and teams of tunnel-diggers—young men lured by the promise of paid employment—who worked tirelessly to dig a 4,921-foot-long tunnel, more than

30 feet beneath the surface.[46] This passage led to an unmarked warehouse, which was used to shield the tunneling activity, about a mile from the prison.[47]

"El Chapo"—Hero or Outlaw

According to a recent *New York Times* report, Guzmán Loera's escape actually "enhanced his status as an outlaw folk hero."[48] Far from condemning his escape, some Mexican villagers in the Sinaloa region had been hopeful that Guzmán Loera's operations would provide more jobs and opportunities to work on his land. The regional economy depended on the Mexican drug trade—and on Guzmán Loera as a leader of that trade. In fact, in February 2014, when police took Guzmán into custody for the second time, the communities that grew marijuana for the Sinaloa Cartel reverted to growing corn, a less profitable commodity.[49] With the possibility of Guzmán Loera's return, the revival of the marijuana farms became a topic on the streets of the Sinaloa mountain towns in the Badiraguato municipality, Guzmán Loera's birthplace.[50]

Some Sinaloa residents reported another benefit of Guzmán Loera's escape: an increased sense of security in the area. These residents felt that Guzmán Loera's presence caused rival gangs to display less violence—something they said the police could not accomplish. In another *New York Times* article, an engineer who had been visiting the area from Mexico City voiced a growing sentiment when he said, "Drug dealers do more for the people than the government does. If you live in a dealer's territory, he treats you well. The government won't do anything for you. It's all bureaucracy and red tape."[51]

El Chapo Recaptured

Early in the morning of January 8, 2016, Guzmán Loera was recaptured in a fierce gun battle just six months after escaping from Altiplano prison. His recapture was the culmination of an extensive manhunt that was the largest anti-drug operation ever undertaken by the Mexican government, involving months of surveillance, every law enforcement agency in the country, and assistance from the U.S.[52]

In early January 2016, Guzmán Loera arrived in Los Mochis, a Pacific coastal town in Sinaloa. The home where he sought refuge had been under surveillance for weeks; Mexican authorities had been led to the region as they followed one of the chief tunnel-diggers from Guzmán Loera's second escape.[53] Authorities had been waiting and watching as construction crews renovated the house; they intercepted cartel communications indicating that "someone big was about to arrive."[54]

Just after midnight on January 8, authorities confirmed that this was the drug cartel boss and his inner circle.

At 4:30 a.m., Special Forces marines from the Mexican Navy descended on the home, where they met resistance from several gunmen in a maze of narrow corridors. The gunfire continued for over an hour, and by 6:30 a.m. the house was deemed secure. Five of Guzmán Loera's henchmen were killed and one Mexican marine wounded in the raid, and the remaining occupants of the house were arrested. But there was no sign of Guzmán Loera.[55]

During the marines' inspection of the home, they discovered that it—like many of Guzmán Loera's homes—was equipped with elaborate escape hatches and tunnels. As the bloody gun battle had raged, Guzmán Loera and his top lieutenant had slipped away through a tunnel behind a closet mirror, which led to the sewer drain. They surfaced a little more than half a mile away outside of Walmart.[56] From there they hijacked a white Volkswagen, and its driver alerted police. When the Volkswagen overheated, they abandoned it and hijacked another.

14 Chapter 2

The federal police apprehended the fugitives on the outskirts of town. Nervous at the thought of "holding two of the deadliest men in all of Mexico" and fearing that cartel forces might try to attempt a rescue, the police thought it best to take the pair to a local hotel while they waited for the marines.[57] Their fear was well-founded, as police were soon alerted that as many as "40 assassins were on their way to free their leader."[58]

Once the marines arrived, Guzmán Loera was taken to Mexico City, where he was "paraded before a field of news cameras" at the airport in Mexico City before being escorted to a helicopter to be returned to Altiplano. The U.S. suggested extraditing Guzmán Loera for trial and that matter remained in discussion with the U.S. The prison authorities assured government officials that they "would rotate his cells, never allowing him to stay anywhere long enough to burrow his way out again."[59]

By noon on January 8, Mexico's president, Enrique Pena Nieto, tweeted "Mission accomplished: We have him."[60] For Nieto, now in the fourth year of his presidency, this concluded a humiliating chapter for his administration, which has been laden with a series of security and corruption scandals, including Guzmán Loera's second prison break. Eager to declare success, strengthen his leadership, and possibly accelerate a revival of his popularity, President Nieto released the following statement: "Our security institutions have demonstrated that our citizens can trust them, and they have the stature, strength, and determination to accomplish any mission they are tasked with."[61]

On the other hand, many Mexican citizens were so distrustful of the government that they deemed the detailed account of the escape suspicious and even labeled it "a piece of theater."[62] Some believed that the government itself fabricated the escape story, and that Guzmán Loera had never even been in prison a second time. They claimed the Mexican government was using this escape story as a diversionary tactic to deflect the focus from other issues, such as the "corruption that saturates the government at all levels."[63]

Nor was there agreement as to the desirability of imprisoning Guzmán Loera. The local view was in part that "the Sinaloa Cartel kept order, often more effectively than the government, and that it was even more adept at providing basic security services."[64] Besides homicides and kidnappings having "declined sharply" in the area, many residents of Los Mochis and across the Sinaloa state "credit the cartel with bringing stability through efforts such as building houses, schools, and hospitals in impoverished communities."[65]

Notes

1 Patrick Radden Keefe, "The Snow Kings of Mexico," *The New York Times Magazine*, June 17, 2012, 36.
2 Elida Bustos, "LATIN 500," *Latin Trade*, July/August, Vol. 20, No. 4 (2012): 16–40.
3 Dolia Estevez, "Mexican Drug Kingpin El Chapo Drops Out of Billionaire Ranks," Forbes, March 5, 2013, www.forbes.com/sites/doliaestevez/2013/03/05/mexican-drug-kingpin-el-chapo-out-of-billionaire-ranks/. http://perma.cc/BP2V-MBT3.
4 Patrick Radden Keefe, "How a Mexican Drug Cartel Makes Its Billions," *The New York Times Magazine*, June 15, 2012.
5 Luis Astorga and David A. Shirk, "Drug Trafficking Organizations and Counter-Drug Strategies in the US–Mexican Context," Evolving Democracy, Center for US–Mexican Studies, UC San Diego, 2010. www.escholarship.org/uc/item/8j647429. http://perma.cc/UAX5-C3DV.
6 Jerry Langton, *Gangland: The Rise of the Mexican Drug Cartels from El Paso to Vancouver* (Canada: Wiley, 2011).
7 Ibid.
8 Langton, *Gangland*, 2011; Astorga and Shirk, "Drug Trafficking Organizations," 2010; Keefe, "Snow Kings of Mexico," 2012.

The Sinaloa Cartel as a Concrete Example **15**

9 Langton, *Gangland*, 2011.
10 David Luhnow and Jose De Corboda, "The Drug Lord Who Got Away," *Wall Street Journal*, June 13, 2009. http://online.wsj.com/article_email/SB124484177023110993-lMyQjAxMTIwNDE0ODgxNDgxWj.html#. http://perma.cc/S2TR-UK6S.
11 Luhnow and De Corboda, "The Drug Lord," 2009; Miguel R. Salazar and Eric L. Olson, "A Profile of Mexico's Major Organized Crime Groups," Woodrow Wilson International Center for Scholars. www.wilsoncenter.org/sites/default/files/profile_organized_crime_groups.pdf. http://perma.cc/CPC4-CQX3.
12 Langton, *Gangland*, 2011.
13 Luhnow and De Corboda, "The Drug Lord," 2009.
14 Malcolm Beith, *The Last Narco* (New York: Grove Press, 2010), 17–18.
15 Howard Campbell, *Drug War Zone* (Austin, TX: University of Texas Press, 2009); June S. Beittel, "Mexico's Drug Trafficking Organizations: Source and Scope of the Violence," Congressional Research Service, April 15, 2013. www.fas.org/sgp/crs/row/R41576.pdf. http://perma.cc/NV6D-NRUY.
16 Keefe, "Snow Kings of Mexico," 2012.
17 U.S. Department of the Treasury, "Treasury Designates Sinaloa Cartel Plaza Bosses," May 7, 2013. www.treasury.gov/press-center/press-releases/Pages/jl1927.aspx. http://perma.cc/SB9C-65A4.
18 Tim McGirk, "Mexican Drug Cartels Set Up Show in California Parks," *Time*, August 22, 2009.
19 Keefe, "Snow Kings of Mexico," 2012.
20 Keefe, "Snow Kings of Mexico," 2012; William Finnegan, "The Kingpins," *The New Yorker*, July 2, 2012.
21 See Langton, *Gangland*, 2011.
22 Keefe, "Snow Kings of Mexico," 2012; Beittel, "Mexico's Drug Trafficking Organizations," 2013.
23 Finnegan, "Kingpins," 2012.
24 Michael Kelley, "World Drug Report Reveals the Staggering Extent of North America's Meth Problem," *Business Insider*, June 26, 2013. www.businessinsider.com/north-america-has-a-massive-meth-problem-2013–6. http://perma.cc/HB8Z-GRT4.
25 Finnegan, "Kingpins," 2012.
26 Superseding Indictment at 8, *United States v. Guzmán-Loera, et al.*, No. 09 CR 383 (N.D.Ill February 2, 2008).
27 Beith, *The Last Narco*, 2010, 70.
28 Beith, *The Last Narco*, 2010, 70; Sebastian Rotella, "Food Company Owners Charged in Drug Tunnel Case," *Los Angeles Times*, September 29, 1995.
29 Keefe, "Snow Kings of Mexico," 2012.
30 Ibid.
31 Ibid.
32 Rachel Uranga and Mica Rosenberg, "Tunnels Proliferate Under US–Mexico Border," *The Globe and Mail*, December 12, 2011.
33 Beith, *The Last Narco*, 2010, 70–71.
34 Marc Lacey, "Smugglers of Drugs Burrow on Border," *New York Times*, October 2, 2010.
35 Adam Higgonbottom, "Narco Tunnels of Border Town Nogales Show Sinaloa Cartel's Power," Bloomberg, August 2, 2012.
36 Keefe, "Snow Kings of Mexico," 2012.
37 Ibid.
38 Ibid.
39 Ibid.
40 Jason McGahan, "Why Mexico's Sinaloa Cartel Loves Selling Drugs in Chicago," Chicago Magazine, October 2013.
41 Martin Duran, Elliot Spagat, and Michael Weissenstein, "How Mexican Marines Captured the World's Most Notorious Drug Kingpin," *Business Insider*, February 23, 2014.
42 Ibid.
43 Ibid.

16 Chapter 2

44 Dolia Estevez, "El Chapo Guzman's First Six Months in Prison: No U.S. Extradition Request and a Successful Hunger Strike," *Forbes*, August 21, 2014. www.forbes.com/sites/doliaestevez/2014/08/21/el-chapo-guzmans-first-six-months-in-prison-no-u-s-extradition-request-and-a-successful-hunger-strike/.

45 Monte Reel, "Underworld: How the Sinaloa Drug Cartel Digs Its Tunnels," *The New Yorker*, August 3, 2015.

46 Ibid.

47 Azam Ahmed and Paulina Villegas, "$1 Million Price Tag Hinted at in El Chapo's Escape," *New York Times*, July 16, 2015. www.nytimes.com/2015/07/17/world/americas/1-million-pricetag-hinted-in-el-chapos-escape.html?_r=0.

48 William Neuman and Azam Ahmed, "Public Enemy? At Home in Mexico, 'El Chapo' Is Folk Hero No. 1," *New York Times*, July 17, 2015. www.nytimes.com/2015/07/18/world/americas/safe-haven-for-drug-kingpin-el-chapo-in-many-mexicans-hearts.html.

49 Ibid.

50 The Associated Press, "Key Dates in the Life of Drug Lord 'El Chapo' Guzman," AP.org, July 12, 2015. http://bigstory.ap.org/article/de91a9d55ea84f4394909275b03f3384/key-dates-life-drug-lord-el-chapo-guzman.

51 Neuman and Ahmed, "Public Enemy?" 2015.

52 Azam Ahmed, "El Chapo, Escaped Mexican Drug Lord, is Recaptured in Gun Battle," *New York Times*, January 8, 2016. www.nytimes.com/2016/01/09/world/americas/El-Chapo-captured-mexico.html.

53 Azam Ahmed, "How El Chapo was Finally Captured, Again," *New York Times*, January 16, 2016. www.nytimes.com/2016/01/17/world/americas/mexico-el-chapo-sinaloa-sean-penn.html.

54 Ibid.

55 Ibid.

56 Ibid.

57 Ibid.

58 Ibid.

59 Ibid.

60 "Mexico's Most Wanted Man is Captured—Again," *The Economist*, January 9, 2016. www.economist.com/news/americas/21685730-government-escapes-major-embarrassment-mexicos-most-wanted-man-capturedagain.

61 Azam Ahmed, "Mexico Moves to Extradite Drug Kingpin Called El Chapo to the US," *New York Times*, January 9, 2016. www.nytimes.com/2016/01/10/world/americas/el-chapo-mexico-extradition-united-states.html.

62 William Neuman, "Mexicans Aren't Buying Official Account of 'El Chapo' Escape," *New York Times*, August 5, 2015. www.nytimes.com/2015/08/07/world/americas/mexicans-arent-buying-official-account-of-el-chapo-escape.html.

63 Ibid.

64 Paulina Villegas and Alberto Arce, "An Uncertain New Chapter in Sinaloa, Home State of 'El Chapo,'" *New York Times*, January 10, 2016. www.nytimes.com/2016/01/11/world/americas/an-uncertain-new-chapter-in-sinaloa-el-chapos-home-state.html.

65 Ibid.

3

STRATEGIES FOR A STATE ADDRESSING ORGANIZED CRIME

Discrete Concerns, Broad Goals, and Overall Strategies for a State Addressing Organized Crime

What about the businesses of organized crime is a matter of relatively grave concern to a powerful modern state? There are several answers to that question.

The first is obvious. The activities of organized crime are criminal because the government believes they are harmful. Even if organized crime was totally peaceful and not disruptive of government, the state would want to stop its central activities, whether these focus on the business of selling contraband (like Sinaloa), or the extortion of legal and illegal businesses, or something else.

The second concern is that the organized crime businesses regularly attract violence. The rivalries between cartels based in Sinaloa and those from Tijuana or Juárez were excruciatingly violent and cruel. The explanation may be as simple as the fact that, involving highly profitable illegal activities, competition among providers is nevertheless not controlled by law or law enforcement. In fact, one common part of the structure of organized crime from New York to Naples has been the effort to find a substitute for intramural violence: a wise older leader or a commission that provides some set of rules for the interaction of organized criminal groups and, critically, resolves disputes whose flare-ups into violence would be very bad for everyone's business.

Fierce competition itself may be hard to restrain because of the exceptional profits from, and relative ease of, creating a monopoly in criminal activities. Other factors also fan the flames of violence. Historic enmities and distrust between groups create a quick trigger, as does the danger of law enforcement taking sides. Alliances either with other organized crime groups or with corrupted law enforcement agencies can temptingly, quickly, and lethally tip the scales of cartel powers. Whatever the cause, extreme and repetitive violence has come with the territory in Colombia, Mexico, Italy, Russia, and the United States.

Third, one particular offspring of a capacity for violence—intimidation of participants in law enforcement, from witnesses to judges—imposes, as we shall see, grave costs on a law-respecting society. So does

18 Chapter 3

the fear that can force ordinary citizens to take instructions about demanded or forbidden behavior from unelected wielders of coercive threats.

A fourth major concern is the penetration and capture of governmental institutions and national territories to various extents that run from only the military being able to enter and occupy a territory; to government control and legitimacy shared with the institutions of an organized crime organization; to the infiltration of government organizations through bribes and threats, as many Mexicans believed of the Sinaloa Cartel. All are causes of major concern to a modern state anxious to preserve citizen loyalty to government and commitment to legality. The most common challenge to governance is corruption of line officials (particularly in law enforcement) and the purchase of political influence (often with campaign financing as well as personal payments) over those to whom they report. The assumption of government responsibilities to provide public goods and welfare to win or hold public support for cartel activities in limited territories or businesses is a concern closely related to, and supportive of, a state's loss of control over its own territory and institutions.

Fifth and finally, the state bears the enforcement costs of trying to prevent or control these other costs. Lives, resources, and economic losses are at stake. Policing and imprisonment are expensive. The dangers of a life of violent crime often appear to be a realistic price for the young and poor to pay for the chance of becoming rich or simply living well. The government must bear the costs of deterrence and of counter-offers of work opportunities and services to match those offered by organized crime from Medellin to South Boston.

Each of these is a substantial cause of concern to a state faced with powerful organized crime groups. Their description as separate concerns does not, however, adequately cover the symbolic and legitimacy costs of allowing a direct challenge to the rule of law and the collapse of trust in, and loyalty to, government. The loss of public trust that comes with corruption, the failure or inability to insist on legality from powerful groups, the loss of ordinary citizens' sense of equality of participation or at least of an opportunity to participate in the benefits of the state—all of these severely undermine loyalty to a government and thus weaken its powers to serve its citizens and assure their freedom and sense of security. Nieto's authority was undermined by the apparent ease with which El Chapo escaped from Mexico's most secure prisons.

Three Specific Strategies That, If Successful, Would Reduce These Concerns

The fact that these five concerns are often generated by an OCG does not define a set of concrete goals for the state. Each of the concerns could be addressed in a number of ways—the method of addressing them is part of the strategy of the state—the part that defines goals. There are three broad options for the state in attempting to reduce the concerns created by organized crime.

1. First, the state may make the goal that shapes its strategy to eliminate the organization itself or at least to radically reduce its capacity to continue as a profit-making organization controlling certain areas of both crime and legitimate economic activity. That might correspond to bankrupting a legitimate organization or forcing an unconditional surrender in a war. This type of goal is difficult to realize. Consider the possible bases of a cartel's resiliency to hostile state actions. Its leadership, like Guzmán Loera, could be captured or killed, but the organization could continue much as an American

corporation would survive the death of its CEO. That has been the result in Mexico of pursuing this goal—a result often made worse by wars over who will be the new leader in a particular location. An alternative path to the same goal—to eliminate or deter much of the membership of an organization by capture or killing or deterrence through threats—may be far more difficult than pursuing its leaders; it requires knowing who is working with it and for it and who is waiting to join the organization. Even if government success in destroying key parts of an organization was broadly damaging to the business of a particular organized crime group, if there were attractive business opportunities left behind, new organizations would and do replace the groups that were eliminated. Unless customers no longer seek illegal goods and services, a market in illegal business opportunities would always remain in place.

Thus, defining the government's objective in terms of "eliminating" an organization that is producing this array of concerns may be far less helpful and plausible than it at first appears. The published U.S. strategy wisely limits its goals to reducing the capabilities of organized crime until it is a problem manageable by normal law enforcement.

2. The second alternative—limiting the capacities of organized crime—brings in a new set of players to help control the powers and actions of the organized crime group. It is to change the setting in which the organized crime group operates by bringing in effective and trusted law enforcement units and convincing a supportive and trusting community to assist them. In one sense this goal is far more promising; by changing the involvement and alliances of the players, other than the cartels, it promises a stability and a permanence that cannot be achieved by temporarily mobilizing enough force to destroy one organization in a setting still tempting to any would-be successor. Moreover, the goal is at least as achievable; building and leaving in place the new forces needed to deal with any resurgence of organized crime is a difficult, but far more familiar, task than eliminating the very possibility of new organized crime groups resuming a profitable business.

In places with large, violent criminal organizations, bringing about the entrance of new civilian players who are loyal, competent, and popular may require starting with the determined use of military force against organized crime to embolden citizens and to allow law enforcement to itself combat a less dangerous, remaining organized crime group. But—with community support and an honest, trained law enforcement—success in this goal could be declared sooner, more plausibly, and without the need to completely and permanently destroy what may be a resilient form of economic behavior.

3. The final option is that the state may choose, as its more modest goal, identifying the most dangerous harms generated by a particular form of organized crime and eliminating or reducing the motivation or capacity to create those particular harms while leaving the profitability of other gang activities largely in place. That step could be taken by an explicit or implicit understanding with one or several organized crime groups that the harm of greatest concern—say, violence—will be the focus of government activity. The Mexican PRI is thought to have had such an understanding in earlier decades with the predecessor of the Sinaloa Cartel.

Alternatively, it might involve simply a unilateral decision by the state to raise the costs to the OCG of bringing about those particular harms or eliminating the conditions in which they thrive. Of course, different measures may be more or less effective in reducing the motivation or capacity to create particular harms; and the remedy to reduce one set of harms may simply exacerbate other concerns.

20 Chapter 3

What Focusing on Particular Concerns Would Require

Consider the ways that the third broad path might work with regard to each of the five primary concerns of a government facing powerful organized crime groups. And note what we know about the difficulties of reducing each of those concerns in particular ways.

Reducing illegal drug sales by a cartel. Take, as an example, the powerful Sinaloa Cartel in Mexico and its drug businesses. What could be done to reduce its illegal trade? We might try to reduce the citizen demand for its drugs—very largely in the U.S.—and thereby reduce the harms from drugs and from the use of its revenues to fund corruption, violence, and intimidation. But a series of carefully designed program evaluations has shown that we know very little about how to reduce demand.

The historic record also raises serious questions about how much improved forms of treatment of addicts could reduce use. Still, much of the demand for cocaine or heroin is by addicts who are arrested frequently and create much of the harm of drug abuse. Mandatory testing as a condition of probation of an addict, accompanied by even small, but very certain, penalties for his continued use or for his missing tests, might reduce the total use and harm greatly. Several states have therefore recently experimented, at the urging of Professor Mark Kleiman of New York University, with making minor penalties a nearly certain consequence of continued use after arrest. The initial results are encouraging.

We could try to use law enforcement to make the costs and risks of participating in the drug business so high that it would be impossible for groups like Sinaloa to maintain the profitability of the business while selling at a price attractive to most users. But we haven't had much success in increasing the price or lowering the purity of cocaine despite billions of dollars of increased effort to punish the manufacture, sale, and use of drugs. And success in raising prices would have its costs. Price rises resulting in reduced profits might simply move the business to other legal or illegal operations—for example, from alcohol to narcotic painkillers to kidnapping.

We could disrupt, without destroying, the elaborate retail market for illicit drugs. That has proved successful in the case of street markets that depend on a location safe from arrests of dealers and their customers. Alternatively, without reducing overall drug sales and use we could disrupt the market structures used by one powerful cartel by deflecting supply to other sources that don't have similarly developed practices and relationships. Mexico and the United States could, for example, together try to increase the competition that the seemingly well-organized Sinaloa Cartel faces in selling drugs into the United States by lowering the costs and risks that rivals face in smuggling into the United States. One form of this option could be legalization of the production, transportation, and distribution of one or more illicit drugs in the United States. If, for example, marijuana could be grown and sold legally throughout the United States, Mexican cartels would lose a critical part of their drug business to lower cost providers.

Reducing violence in the drug business; extortion; and the use of threats to enforce certain behaviors on ordinary citizens. There is a different set of options for dealing with violence and fear. We could target law enforcement on the violent activities of drug trafficking organizations, hoping to make the costs of their use of violence greater than its benefits. We could try to increase the danger and cost of acquiring, carrying, and using weapons. Or we could focus the anti-drug activities of the Mexican and U.S. government on the most violent groups.

Although there are significant legitimacy risks, the government could use the power of a second cartel in this effort. It could support one organized crime group against its rivals and then bring all of the government forces to bear on a bargain with that remaining group. The regulatory terms of the accommodation could make the survival of the chosen cartel dependent upon a substantial responsiveness to government demands in terms of choosing what forms of illegal business it will engage in and how it is to be carried out (e.g., with less violence and less threat of violence). Many think this was the strategy adopted by the PRI party in Mexico in the last decades of the 20th century when violence was far less severe a problem of drug dealing.

Reducing "capture" of government and the resulting loss of state legitimacy. We could address the capture of governmental institutions, particularly in Mexico, by vigorous law enforcement and systems of administrative monitoring against corruption and intimidation at an operating level, and by cutting off or reducing the forms of purchase of political influence at high levels (such as campaign contributions). However, while the benefits to this tactic are potentially great, the task is daunting in practice. For the loss of citizens' belief in the legitimacy of a government unable to control organized crime, the only answer may be the development of institutions that can demonstrate the effectiveness and the universality of the application of the rule of law to crime, the resolution of civil disputes, and tax collection. That may require developing new law enforcement units with new legal powers and new criminal statutes and providing adequate levels of services, security, and justice—measures taken as efforts to convince the public that the government itself is worth supporting. Chicago and New York traveled this path in the years since 1960, departing from traditions and expectations of corruption and of willingness to share governance with organized crime.

The costs and prospects of these types of concern-reducing measures. We would have to consider the costs, in terms of each of our concerns, of any measure that looked promising in terms of reducing another. Not only may reducing one concern increase others (reducing drug trafficking may well increase violent extortion as a profit-making alternative) but particular steps to deal with one concern may prove unexpectedly counterproductive (stopping the smuggling from Colombia of one bulky drug, marijuana, led to a shift to exporting a far less bulky but far more dangerous drug, cocaine).

How Serious is the Threat Posed by the Activities of Organized Crime?

These are the primary concerns associated with organized crime, but how serious is the overall threat that organized crime poses? In the words of the U.S. National Security Council, that depends primarily on whether the OCG has girded itself with impunity and durability by "a pattern of corruption and/or violence ... [or] protecting their illegal activities through a transnational organizational structure and the exploitation of transnational commerce or communication mechanisms." When an OCG has developed these capacities, the United States National Security Council defines it as a national security threat—a concern of the highest order. That characterization, suggesting extreme danger, may mislead.

Labeling an OCG a "national security threat" can have either of two purposes, each of which seems only applicable to *some* organized crime, even in the relatively dangerous form we have described. At a minimum, the White House calls transnational organized crime a national security threat to note that it is still beyond the normal powers of law enforcement to control. That has been true in Mexico, in Colombia, in Italy, and elsewhere. The National Security Council strategy reflects this meaning when it describes as its goal "to reduce transnational organized crime (TOC) from a national security threat to a manageable public safety problem in the United States and in strategic regions around the world."

But, this has been accomplished domestically in the United States and that accomplishment is not threatened in any significant way by organized crime in Mexico and other countries, in major part

22 Chapter 3

because the normal powers of law enforcement in the United States were expanded in careful ways for the very purpose of giving it the capacity to deal with organized crime.

The second meaning of a "national security threat" is that transnational organized crime, like terrorism or proliferation of weapons of mass destruction, endangers the very existence of our political system, or the independence of our nation, or the continued safety and well-being of a significant portion of our population and institutions. This, too, is untrue for organized crime in the United States at this time, although it may be true for Guatemala or even parts of Mexico.

The National Security Council's exaggeration of the level of threat posed by organized crime would be unimportant except for the political danger that comes with the label "national security threat." Although none of the following are recommended (or repudiated) in the U.S. strategy, the concept of a national security threat has frequently eased the path for the use of the military to deal with a problem involving competitive violence. It has suggested an occasion for what other nations call "emergency powers," on the ground that ordinary law and democratic decision-making are too slow and too protective of civil liberties and property rights to be effective against the threat. Politically, calling something a "national security threat" narrows the range of options that will be considered and the number of people considering them, focusing citizens and officials on forceful means and confrontation. It discourages consideration of costs because of its suggestion that failure to bear them endangers very basic levels of security.

A president's designating something a national security threat has cost us dearly in the past. In the case of Iraq, it has justified a willingness to go to war, in a situation where the legislature might not otherwise support a war. It has generally been the explanation for authorizing behavior—such as waterboarding or drone strikes on uncertain targets in foreign countries or detention of individuals who have never been accorded a judicial trial—that would not be politically acceptable and possible without the "national security" justification. It has justified the monitoring of vast amounts of data from every electronic communication and perhaps every record of an individual's business activities in the United States.

A nation's response to organized crime must be far more textured. *Some* forms of ongoing organized crime in *some* places at *some* times can threaten to undermine much of the basis of citizen acceptance of the legitimacy of a liberal democratic government. Even if it faces such a threat, a government must determine whether or not the present law enforcement system or a strengthened law enforcement system can adequately deal with the threat posed by organized crime. Further, organized crime may or may not present a danger to our institutional or personal safety requiring an extraordinary response. Regardless of the National Security Council designation, the United States seems quite capable of dealing with any remaining organized crime problem within its territory by a set of law enforcement measures that we will describe at some length in Chapter 7.

Undefined and unspecified fear attaches to the term "organized crime" much as it attaches to the word "terrorism." A responsible approach to organized crime must begin with a far more detailed understanding of how it operates, under what constraints, with what dangers to governments and their citizens. It must also ask how governments can respond—either using law enforcement or using emergency powers and national security agencies. If law enforcement is to be the tool of the response, a careful understanding of its capacity to address organized crime requires assessing the vulnerabilities of both law enforcement and organized crime and the steps, like those the United States has taken, that can enable law enforcement to meet the challenges of corruption and intimidation and to develop a new, more resilient style of investigation and prosecution.

Finally, assessing the problem adequately in the 21st century requires looking at how nations may address the difficulties that state boundaries pose for law enforcement, that is, the challenges of globalization of organized crime. For a definition to serve its final purpose of having the capacity to describe what to expect from the activities of the organization we will have to expand it in the next chapter by addressing a set of additional questions. To warrant widespread fear and the major national effort it generates, the criminal organization must have certain capacities and must be able to use them to organize and conduct the illegal business without the help of law or government or the broad social understandings that facilitate needed cooperation for a legal business; and it must have the capacity to displace and/or stave off the attacks of rivals seeking to displace its businesses by the use of force. Finally, to deal with governments it must have the contacts and financing necessary for effective, continuing, large-scale corruption. To deal with law enforcement it must have the capacity to maintain fear and guarantee secrecy.

4

A FINAL ISSUE OF STATE STRATEGY

Rules of War or Law Enforcement

The role of organized crime in the political economy of the state, and the "business" strategies that role invites or requires of an organized crime group, make powerful and uncontrolled organized crime groups the source of serious concerns for a state from which they operate. These include: uncontrolled crimes of dealing in contraband and extortion; violence strongly associated with competition among rival groups for profits from those crimes; infiltration and shared control of critical government institutions if not of territory; the heavy costs of combating organized crime; and, above all, the loss of public support for, and loyalty to, the government.

We have seen that there are three primary goals governments have in addressing this problem. They can attempt to destroy or reduce the capacities of the organizations; or to create law enforcement institutions and a civil society that is capable of diminishing the impact of organized crime over time; or to focus on alleviating specific concerns by, for example, creating incentives for less violent and threatening behavior by the criminal groups. For each of these governmental goals, we have articulated a number of possible steps (sometimes inconsistent with the simultaneous pursuit of a different goal or the reduction of a different concern).

The state needs a strategy for deciding which of the broad goals, or which of the specific concerns listed in the last chapter, it should pursue first and in what ways. The state must consider sequence, for it may be necessary first to attack with maximum military force an organized crime organization that controls a city in order to regain sufficient control of the streets; only then can government make possible the building of law enforcement and civil society. This was true for Mexico in regaining control in the city of Juárez in the last decade. In other words, a government needs an intelligent plan for deciding what tasks, leading to what goals, need to be accomplished in what sequence.

There are, moreover, two very basic questions that will also enter into the strategy and its prospects for success in addressing the goals or concerns for which it is designed. (1) If the organized crime group is powerful, threatening, and uncontrolled, the state must consider the costs and benefits of each of four major forces available to a state for dealing with national security dangers—the military, intelligence agencies, foreign assistance, and domestic law enforcement. And (2) the state must also decide what, if any, system of rules is applicable to whichever form of force is to be used. Let us start with the choice among systems of rules.

Choosing the Applicable System of Rules

The more unconstrained the rules the government accepts for use of its forces, the more likely it is to be able to do severe damage to an organized crime group, as Colombia did to its most dangerous cartels. This, however, comes at the risk of losing the forms of social support it needs from its citizens: trust, cooperation, and loyalty. The more a government remains bound to the rules of law enforcement when dealing with the most serious forms of crime, the more long-term public support it may engender, but at the risk of finding itself outgunned by crime.

The Choice to Bypass the Familiar Protections of Domestic Law

The joint effort by the military and intelligence forces of Colombia and the United States and their private allies, legitimate and illegitimate, to destroy the Medellin Cartel of Pablo Escobar was largely unconstrained by rules of law. While the Medellin Cartel thrived, Pablo Escobar seemed untouchable. He could not be found to be arrested. His forces could outgun those of the government. When key associates were arrested and there was serious talk about extradition to the United States, bombs would go off in Bogotá and elsewhere; judges and ministers would be assassinated. When he was eventually imprisoned, bribing the prison guards assured Escobar that he could walk away when and if, despite being provided every convenience and comfort, he wanted to leave the prison.

The leaders of the forces against him or their families were targeted for assassination by the Medellin Cartel, as were judges, ministers, and prosecutors. Much of the Colombian Supreme Court was killed for its role in authorizing extradition. Much of the Congress was bribed to pass a constitutional amendment forbidding extradition. Without extradition, trials in Colombia seemed hopelessly subject to threats, bribes, and the murder of witnesses.

Colombia responded to this massive intimidation, corruption, and violence by Escobar and the Medellin Cartel: changing court procedures to include trials where the identity of judges and witnesses could be kept secret; appointing a new prosecutor of organized crime and housing his operation in highly secure facilities; and developing schemes of witness protection and judicial protection. But still Escobar and the Medellin Cartel continued to thrive and to control much of law enforcement.

The government gained traction against Medellin only when Colombia's military and special police units combined forces with powerful U.S. operational units for electronic intelligence operations, on-the-ground assistance of the U.S. Drug Enforcement Administration, and the CIA. Even then, to target Escobar, locating and killing him required the alliance to recruit Escobar's organized crime and paramilitary rivals in Colombia, particularly the Cali Cartel. The combined team was allowed to become a force as ruthless as Escobar's forces but far more powerful. Everyone associated with the Medellin Cartel was threatened with assassination. Many were killed. Escobar himself was killed in his hideaway in Bogotá after his organization had been devastated by assassinations and the massive defection of his frightened associates.

The forces and alliances unleashed on Escobar and the Medellin Cartel were similar to the forces and alliances the U.S. later developed for counter-terrorism against terrorist threats in South Asia. There, the special wartime measures allowed by the law of war replaced domestic law enforcement but without the special protections of individuals that the law of war also required. More precisely, gaping holes were left in wartime rights of combatants who were terrorists wherever, under the law of war, protection required openly identifying oneself as a member of a foreign military. Much the same rules were applied to the Medellin Cartel but almost wholly without the ameliorative procedures gradually developed by the United States over time to moderate the initial set of rules in South Asia. Even compared to a "war" against Al-Qaeda, where those reasonably suspected of providing it support could be targeted for killing, detained for an indefinite period, or subjected to a military trial and where torture or near-torture was used for a time, the rules of the forces attacking Escobar were less careful, precise, and humane. All this seemed necessary to eliminate a murderous rival to the authority of the Colombian state.

The uses of force which are most threatening not only to the organized crime organization, but, incidentally and collaterally, to the public and to its loyalty to the state are the powers to kill, detain, surveil, and interrogate without judicial supervision. The state is at its most intimidating when these activities are not controlled by systems designed to distinguish active adversaries from others ranging from the wholly uninvolved through the passively supportive—including families of those actively involved—and on to those professionally assisting (lawyers and doctors) and only finally to the perpetrators of violence themselves. In the final stages of the Escobar case, there was no recognizable system of rules limiting the state. Individuals all along the chain of complicity with Escobar were threatened with violence at the discretion of those controlling the use of military force and intelligence without the constraints of any system of rules, even the law of warfare.

What was done against Medellin was not justified as compliant with either rules of law enforcement or the rules of war. Moreover, the United States, a foreign participant, was given a freer rein in that Colombian battle than it enjoyed in any other battle against organized crime; so was the Cali Cartel, the most powerful rival of the Medellin Cartel.

Although these measures did reestablish much of the Colombian government's control of the nation, they did not end the drug business which largely funded the Medellin Cartel. The Cali Cartel, formerly the ally of Colombia and the U.S. against Medellin, became the beneficiary of the new opportunities in the drug business, at least until it became the next target of Colombia and the United States. After Cali's influence waned, smaller successors picked up the business. After decades of concerted effort to damage or destroy it, the Colombian industry of manufacturing and distributing cocaine has not been significantly reduced.

The Alternative Decision to Accept and Apply to Organized Crime Most of the Protections of Criminal Law and of the International Law of Human Rights

Mexico has rejected any consideration of organized crime as engaged in a form of warfare against the state. It has adopted a new constitution which reduces the possibilities of developing heightened powers for law enforcement confronted with organized crime; and has limited the foreign assistance of the United States to intelligence, equipment, training, and advice. U.S. agents cannot carry guns in Mexico. It vigorously rejects the notion that organized crime is a form of terrorism, which might make lawful whatever special rules of law enforcement "on steroids" are sometimes applicable elsewhere in terrorist cases. Whether it, in fact, insists on compliance with the rules of law enforcement in violent situations or in pursuing cartel leaders is less than clear.

Other states, like Great Britain, have also continued to rely on law enforcement powers (much as they would be applied to other criminal groups that are not involved in terrorism). Even dealing with terrorist groups, some of our European allies, such as France, have simply added muscle to the normal rules of law enforcement, creating a "law enforcement on a low dose of steroids." The same rules could be applied to any significant threat by organized crime. They are considered adequate to deal with an organized crime group of unusual capacity and determination to resist the state's law, to undermine state authority, and to impose its own will on segments of the population or some part of the territory of the state. The choice of the United States for bolstered rules of law enforcement is described in detail in Chapter 6.

The Israeli system of rules for dealing with terrorism was largely created by its Supreme Court and was not made to depend in the same way as U.S. counter-terrorism on an individual's identification as a member of a foreign military group. Based on the international rules for occupied territories, it is a form of "law of war-lite," often making extraordinary state powers depend upon an ongoing or planned set of attacks by the terrorist organization. This approach could be, but has not been, applied to organized crime as well.

Choosing Applicable Instruments of State Force

The applicable system of rules does not determine what form of organization—the military, the intelligence, or law enforcement—is to be used by the state. The questions are separable. The military or intelligence agencies can be told that in a particular circumstance they are bound by the unfamiliar and limiting rules of law enforcement. Alternatively, the police can be told that, in a particular circumstance, the general constraints on law enforcement are relaxed or eliminated. Still, the decision as to which force is to be used is important.

Forces are trained in the tactics and imbued with the mores of either war or intelligence or law enforcement. Telling any force to operate under an unfamiliar system of rules is likely to create a hybrid set of rules in practice, as well as confusion and resentment. For example, despite the wishes of the Attorney General and the White House, the FBI refused to violate traditional law enforcement rules and take part in highly coercive interrogation of foreign terrorists. Conversely, intelligence agents of every country are trained in how to break the rules of foreign nations or international law abroad, not in how to comply. These teachings survive in new contexts, as exemplified by the early illegal stages of NSA wiretapping ordered by President Bush and Vice President Cheney soon after 9/11.

In dealing with organized crime, in a form admittedly far less threatening than in Mexico, the United States and other modern democratic states have relied on law enforcement forces within much the same boundaries granted, and constraints imposed, for dealing with any crime. Indeed, the United States has treated as quasi-constitutional a statute passed in 1878 as part of the end of Reconstruction after the Civil War. The Posse Comitatus Act of June 18, 1878, forbids, with some exceptions, the use of military force in law enforcement matters. It remains, in the final analysis, only a statute and not a constitutional provision, and so it can be, and has been, amended to create exceptions for severe emergencies threatening the enforcement of the Constitution. Still, it is revered and stands more than 135 years later. The underlying notion of the Act is that the military should not be expected or trusted to enforce the law as it should be enforced: with great respect for the civil liberties of citizens. This tradition remains as a deeply held commitment in the United States.

There are costs to this tradition. Law enforcement's raw powers are limited by a set of rules which are generally inapplicable to the activities of an army. Law enforcement has to work among a set of institutions—courts, prosecutors, other federal and local police agencies—whose cooperation it needs and must win by exercising restraint. As a result, it is less feared and sometimes less respected than the

28 Chapter 4

military which enjoys the popular loyalty that comes with providing protection from foreign enemies. The military is better organized and equipped for the use of massive force than is the police. The foreign intelligence agencies of a state are more accustomed to working closely with the military. In Mexico, for example, what could have been a far more prolonged and bloody battle against dangerous organized crime groups seeking to control the streets of Juárez became one-sided when the military arrived.

The advantage of law enforcement is that it has daily contact with members of the community who may—if they identify with and trust the police, prosecutors, and courts—provide badly needed information about who is planning, or has executed, what crimes. At its best, any policing institution benefits from its recognition that, to maintain the cooperation and support of the public, it has to depend on showing respect for the public and for the liberties of citizens. Maintaining this form of respect is often far more a police tradition than a military tradition. Law enforcement is also trained to gather and hold evidence in particular, required ways so that it is much better able to provide what is reliable and needed at trials.

The training and traditions of the institution must be considered in deciding what tasks it will be asked to perform. Still, general rules may have to give way in novel situations. In Juárez, the military was more trusted as an uncorrupted force than the municipal police. In the United States, as in many other countries, law enforcement has developed a "SWAT" capacity to engage substantial armed opposition in pursuing law enforcement missions.

Alliances

As the Colombian battle against Escobar's Medellin Cartel demonstrates, whether its decision is to use the military or law enforcement as its primary instrument of force, a state can rely in part on the supplemental activities of a foreign state that is also concerned about the organized crime group. As illustrated by the relationship between Mexico and the United States in the first decades of the 21st century, there is a rich variety of forms of assistance. Foreign law enforcement can, through the use of extradition, offer trials in courts that are not intimidated and prosecutors who are better trained than those of the foreign state. This may be necessary to try El Chapo. It can provide training and equipment needed for investigation, prosecution, trial, and imprisonment. Foreign intelligence agencies can gather intelligence by electronic surveillance or overhead flights or informants within one or the other state. The military can furnish helicopters, guns, training, and more.

U.S. assistance to Mexico has recently shifted from emphasizing the military toward emphasizing law enforcement. Which form of assistance, like its companion question, what institution of state power shall be used by the government seeking assistance, depends very much on the goals and concerns identified by the state actors. Assisting the Mexican military to provide an umbrella of safety for the public under which civil society and law enforcement can start to regain confidence and trust may be a necessary starting place even if the state's ultimate goal is helping to build an independent law enforcement structure.

Besides assistance from a foreign government, one other force is available to a state threatened by powerful, lethal, uncontrolled organized crime groups. As we have seen, the groups are likely to have rivals. Mexico had by 2016 identified at least 16 significant cartels—well-armed, highly motivated, and unconstrained by any system of rules of conflict. Rival organized crime groups can have a very powerful effect on the outcome of a struggle between an organized crime group and whatever military, intelligence, or police force is attempting to rein it in. As in Boston in the days of Whitey Bulger (described in

Chapter 9), one organization, Bulger's Winter Hill Gang, often has considerable information about the dealings of a rival gang, in that instance, the Italian Mafia. The Cali Cartel in Colombia had the military force and the freedom from moral or legal constraints to do immense damage to the Medellin Cartel while temporarily enjoying the support and protection of the state.

For Mexico, attempting to eliminate the extremely brutal Zetas, it was helpful to have the assistance of their opponents.

5

DETECTING VISIBLE INDICATIONS OF ORGANIZED CRIME

Introduction

Sales of drugs and extortion may take place frequently for some time and yet remain invisible to law enforcement. Complainants are unlikely and locations for the transactions are carefully chosen to avoid observation. What other patterns of organized crime activity might be used to detect such invisible crimes?

An illegal business (such as selling Colombian cocaine) must take steps to deal with types of threats that a legal business (such as selling Colombian coffee) need not consider. Some are posed by law enforcement and some by rivals for the resources an illegal business needs for profit and security (including ways and routes of smuggling, of money laundering, and of forming alliances with other cartels or the police). The special steps the OCG takes will often produce recognizable patterns of organized crime.

What is constant among, and unique to, OCGs is their need to deal with two major problems. (1) They have to address the problem of government efforts to use law enforcement or security forces against organized crime. That requires taking visible steps to avoid secret forms of surveillance. (2) An OCG has to simultaneously address the danger posed by well-armed rivals. In addition, ways of dealing with smaller threats, such as theft or informants, also leave detectable traces.

The Signs of Illegality: Activities and Capacities

The law enforcement of a state combating organized crime must learn to see those patterns of business activity and of capacity-building that characterize organized crime and no other businesses.

The most obvious pattern, but one difficult to observe, is the focus on familiar illegal money-making activities. Organized crime has come to concentrate on two broad businesses: the sale of contraband goods and services (from trafficking drugs to trafficking humans to selling child pornography); and extortion by selling "protection" against the threats an OCG can create for a legal or marginally legal or illegal business. These two businesses continue to characterize organized crime although there are others: from stealing oil from pipelines in Mexico to renting access points to a profitable market or buying assistance

Visible Indications of Organized Crime **31**

for smuggling or money laundering, and on to using fear to gain control of the Treasury or the pension funds of a labor union.

The choice of the two leading businesses combines safety from detection with profitability. Both are, for different reasons, crimes unlikely to be reported. The buyer of contraband wants the product and the continuing relationship with the seller. The victim of extortion is warned of the severity of the dangers he faces if he reports the threat requiring "protection" by the OCG, and there is not likely to be any other observer to the transaction. As to profitability, that is assured by the government eliminating almost all competition in the market for contraband; and, in the case of extortion, success requires nothing more than choosing a wealthy, poorly guarded target and then conveying the severity and credibility of the threat that accompanies the demand for money. (Credibility may be the greatest problem, for the target can quickly improve its defenses.)

Much of the strategy of an organized crime group depends on being able to prevent its activities from being observed by law enforcement. Much of the success of law enforcement against organized crime, in turn, depends on penetrating OC secrecy by use of a set of forms of secret surveillance: surreptitious electronic or physical surveillance, undercover agents participating in purchases of contraband, or using the threat of conviction and a long sentence to "force" cooperation by either a one-time witness or a continuing informant.

To meet the danger surveillance poses to an OC business engaged in drug distribution and extortion, it must avoid many of the ways ordinary business is carried out and instead adopt alternatives, that, being unusual for business activities, can themselves tip off law enforcement. Forms of money laundering, for example, are necessary to prevent law enforcement from using large unexplained money transfers as a tip-off; but, if detected, the discovered traces of systematic money laundering reveals organized crime. Electronic surveillance can be avoided by not using phones or the Internet and instead meeting in person with co-conspirators, but only at a significant cost in efficiency and in creating observable and suspicious alternative forms of needed communication.

The Traces Left By Corruption and Intimidation

Over time secrecy is likely to fail. So the surest way to protect an illegal business for years or even decades is to develop special capacities to deal with the consequences of successful surveillance. The U.S. National Security Council noted three.

If the OCG, through bribery, can corruptly buy a trustworthy commitment from law enforcement officials or their political leaders to ignore OC's businesses or, better yet, to attack those of its rivals, it need not fear surveillance, arrest, prosecution or prison. If it can develop the capacity and credibility to use fear, it can prevent insiders from becoming witnesses or informants or thieves. Building a capacity to generate loyalty of employees and of members of a community will have the same effect.

Consider the Whitey Bulger case in Boston, described at greater length in Part Two. By providing information about Boston's Italian mafia, Bulger not only helped defeat a formidable rival to his Irish gang (the Italian leader, Jerry Angiulo, was sent to prison for 45 years), but more important, he advanced the career of a grateful FBI agent, John Connolly, who was becoming more and more famous and admired for his role in U.S. attacks on Italian organized crime. By also paying that agent, Connolly, hundreds of thousands of dollars for looking the other way and for bringing the agents and prosecutors working on organized crime in Boston to look the other way, Bulger was buying invaluable help in various forms for his OCG. Once the FBI agent was plainly involved in this corrupt relationship, the

32 Chapter 5

threat of revelation guaranteed that he could not fail to act on Bulger's behalf even if the flow of informational and monetary benefits had stopped.

Bulger's criminal business provided South Boston's bookmaking, loan-sharking, and drugs while extorting heavy payments from legitimate local businesses. What did Bulger's cash and other support for Connolly do for the business? The rewards in deflecting law enforcement were immense. Caught dead to right, he was nonetheless protected from being charged for race-fixing; he was tipped off about wiretaps and aided by information from Connolly in carrying out multiple murders of those Bulger feared might be, or become, government informants against him. All these rewards of corruption could be visible.

Bulger's FBI allies doctored reports and insisted that investigations and prosecutions be dropped on the ground that Bulger's great value as a secret informant against the Italian gangsters would be compromised. Bulger was furnished information about witnesses and informants; he was warned so he could take steps to discourage complainants. When, finally, law enforcement made a solid case against Bulger and his associates despite the obstacles Connolly had thrown in the way, Connolly tipped off Bulger in time for him to escape and successfully hide for decades. This, too, ultimately raised suspicions.

The patterns associated with corruption may be difficult for outsiders to discover especially if the law enforcement that is corrupted for this purpose is willing to protect its position by thwarting government efforts to prosecute the OCG. Still, in due course the pattern would show, at the very least, a number of successful surveillance operations against rivals and a number of failed operations against the Bulger OCG, which was using law enforcement or political influence to destroy its rival. That pattern, too, is relatively unmistakable.

Detectable Traces of Exploitation of International Law: Transnational Operations

A final observation by the U.S. National Security Council is important. OC can also be protected over a prolonged period by the fact that international law prohibits one state (e.g., the state where people are harmed by buying and using cocaine) from engaging in law enforcement in a second state (e.g., where the cocaine is manufactured) without the second state's consent. Important traces of organized criminal activity are likely to be located in the state in which the activity has been organized or is planned and the first steps were taken. But if that state is not harmed by the activity, is indifferent to its prosecution, and cares little about the anger of the other state, those important traces will not be the subject of surveillance by any state.

The Detectable Traces Left By Unrestrained Competition: Killings and Building the Capacities for Warfare

The other threat that only an OCG faces—the threat from rival cartels—creates special patterns of observable capacity and activity. Start with the patterns created by capacities needed for dealing with this threat. To defend its access points and routes for smuggling an OCG may need a reputation for a willingness and capacity to engage in violent, ruthless and terrifying forms of conflict; a network of alliances with other cartels, street gangs, and corrupt law enforcement forces; a well-armed and trained fighting force; and a large dollar reserve to pay for these. Consider the clues left by the battle for Juárez, Mexico, and for the access it provided to the U.S. market for drugs.

Juárez As An Example

Trade between Juárez and the United States exceeds $42 billion or 15 percent of the total trade between the United States and Mexico. Drugs can easily pass through that border, hidden among such a volume of legitimate traffic. Many workers from throughout Mexico unsuccessfully seek jobs in the maquiladora industry of Juárez; they provide a constant supply of recruits for narcotic traffickers. The border industry also provides equipment useful for transportation of drugs across the border and amply supports the banking, communications, and legal institutions drug cartels require. These factors and its proximity to El Paso have made Juárez a highly significant "plaza" or crossing point for smuggled drugs. Somewhere between 1.5 and 10 million dollars' worth of illicit drugs are thought to cross the border every day.

When Mexican routes and entrepreneurs replaced Colombian smugglers in handling Colombian cocaine, the Juárez Cartel became a massive and powerful OCG. But the unexpected death of the leader Amado Carrillo Fuentes in 1997 led to internal divisions and defections to other cartels, leaving a temptingly weakened OCG in control of a rich plaza which a rival cartel, Sinaloa, coveted. Sinaloa was then at war with the Gulf Cartel for a drug route in Nuevo Laredo but when that conflict was settled in 2007, moved in on Juárez. In the next four years of battle, homicides in Juárez grew from 301 each year to 3116 each year, making it the most dangerous city in the world.

The Sinaloa and Juárez Cartels each had drug-selling street gangs as allies, loyal distributors, and soldiers. Each cartel chose violent terror as a tactic to discourage the other. In 2010, the street gang allies of the Juárez Cartel horrified the nation by gunning down 16 people, mostly teenagers, mistakenly believing that the birthday party they attacked was a gathering of Sinaloa's street gang allies.

The Juárez municipal police and mercenaries from the police initially supported the Juárez Cartel. The leader of the police mercenary group supporting Juárez admitted to participating in 1500 murders, including the "birthday party." Sinaloa responded with its "soldiers": the enforcers it uses to maintain the level of violence and fear needed to enforce agreements, protect its property, and discourage informers. Sinaloa used intimidation, bribery, and targeted assassinations to successfully purge the Juárez allies in the municipal police.

Peace returned with President Calderón's strategy of dispatching, in sequence: soldiers, then federal police, then economic assistance to Juárez. Finally, he turned law enforcement over to a somewhat vetted and reformed municipal police, control of which had been given to a new, very tough, chief Leyzaola, whose frightening and forceful tactics had resulted in a remarkable success in an almost equally difficult situation in Tijuana.

There were other possibilities to explain Sinaloa's victory. Some have pointed out that only one in fifty of the people detained for organized crime between 2004 and 2010 were members of the Sinaloa Cartel, suggesting the support Sinaloa was enjoying from the authorities. Sinaloa, in control of Juárez, went on to then battle the Zeta Cartel elsewhere.

As to activities unique to OC, the signs of an ongoing war are, of course, unmistakable to law enforcement and third parties. The object of the warfare generally is to obtain or retain advantages in the processes of buying, manufacturing, transporting, smuggling and selling a much sought-after illegal good or service. The rate of violent deaths increases rapidly and apparently in response to attacks from the rival. As in the Juárez example, the violence is an important part of the contest and dramatic enough to spread terror. The parties are likely to try to draw in government forces and cartel allies. This effort may be observable, too, as it was in the apparent law enforcement support, first, for the Juárez Cartel and, then, for Sinaloa.

34 Chapter 5

Organizational Form, Finance, and Strategy

Three broad characteristics of organized criminal organizations—strategy, structure, and finance—also differ markedly from those of legitimate businesses. But so little is known about what form they take in various OCGs that any consistency of patterns is difficult to use. Books, records and reports of insiders—discovered on rare occasions—provide what we now know.

We know that the Colombian Cali Cartel, at the height of its immense success in 1993—with revenues of about $7 billion—divided itself into five operating divisions. The structure is described by William Rempel in his book, "At the Devil's Table," recounting the life of a Cali Cartel insider, Jorge Salcedo. Each division—trafficking, finance, politics, legal, and military—operated under the supervision of the cartel's senior godfather, Miguel Rodriguez Orejuelai.

"Trafficking" covered warehousing drugs and their distribution to the United States and Europe as well as moving currency back to Cali. "Finance" included not only accounting and monitoring cash flow but making such payments as those to the families of arrested traffickers. The "Politics" division was the lobbying arm of Cali. Included in that activity were courting and paying cash to public officials.

The "Legal" division worked with American lawyers in defending traffickers in the United States as well as providing defense in Colombia. An important ancillary function, according to Rempel and Salcedo, was to convey very clear messages to anyone who was arrested about the price his family would pay if he provided information to the government.

The final division, "Military," included internal security, intelligence, and enforcement. Both the intelligence collection, particularly from law enforcement officials, and the analysis of that information were expensive and extraordinarily thorough. The "Military" also bore responsibility for corrupt payments to police and army personnel which amounted to $20,000/month for Cali policemen and $60,000/month for national police. According to the authors, "By 1993, 1/3 of the police and military in Cali, Medellin, and Bogotá were on the drug cartel's payroll." The military division was also responsible for assassinations both in the United States and in Colombia by sicarios—paid gunmen. Assassinations abroad could cost as much as $100,000 each.

Almost two decades later the books of the Zetas in Mexico were uncovered. The organization had an income of $350 million, mostly from the sale of cocaine and a lively trade in extortion. The Zetas spent much of their time and resources in violent conflict with competitors, even though each recognized that such "wars" were extremely costly in lost lives, lost revenues, and expenses to equip and man an "army." A leader of the Zetas, Jesus Enrique Regon Aguilar, testified that almost all of the $350 million earned in 2010 and most of his personal wealth of $50 million were consumed in a war against the Gulf Cartel, which was itself only a prelude to wars against the Sinaloa Cartel and others. Similarly, Levitt and Venkatesh document through the books of a drug-dealing Chicago street gang the financial battering and the extraordinary risk to members' lives that accompany an attempt to take over territory, or to resist such an attempt. War among organized crime groups seems common, constant, costly, and only partially explicable in economic terms.

One difference revealed by the seized accounting records is especially revealing of the differences in the governmental settings facing the Chicago gang, on the one hand, and the Zeta Cartel, on the other. The account books of the U.S. street gang show no category for corruption of politicians, law enforcement officials, or judges. Payments to bribe army and police officers were a very prominent "line item" in the books of the Zeta Cartel. The cost bought information, assistance, and enforcement activity targeting members of other cartels.

Patterns of Routine Operations

A criminal organization is characterized by more than its structure and finances. It typically has an understanding of how best to turn its capacities into a set of plans for carrying out a profit-making business. To develop this set of plans it must take account of all the answers to a set of questions identifying the nature of its central relationships. The overall plan for using capacities and resources, activities and precautions, to conduct a particular business (most frequently the sale of illegal goods and services or of "protection") creates a strategic pattern that may well be visible to law enforcement.

A legitimate business and an organized crime business are likely to have to address a somewhat similar set of questions in making an overall plan. Each needs a strategy. But the differences in the situation—in particular the unique threats to an organized crime business—will produce quite different answers to the same fundamental questions. A company buying, processing, transporting, and selling Colombian coffee will, for example, have a very different relationship to government in the states where it operates from those a drug cartel confronts. The nature of competition and other critical relationships will also be very different. Thus the answers to the same set of questions about relationships important to the business will point to strategies. Sinaloa must find, exploit, and protect a set of advantages in a business that requires avoiding law enforcement while both deflecting rivals and selling its product to individuals eager to obtain it.

1. Who are the competitors in providing goods or services and what effect does this competition have on the business of the particular OCG or the coffee company (CC) being examined?
    a. What are the products being manufactured, transported, and sold? For the coffee seller, it is coffee; for an OCG, like Sinaloa, it is illegal drugs or "protection."
    b. What is the competitive advantage of the organization? The quality of the product is a likely answer for the CC; superiority in capacity for smuggling, for Sinaloa.
    c. What is the nature of the competitive challenge? For the CC it is likely to be price or quality; for Sinaloa it may be capacity in warfare.
2. Who are the suppliers of needed materials to the organization?
    a. For the CC, open plantations; for Sinaloa, secret growers and processors who are themselves violating the law.
    b. What is the nature of the formal and informal relationships with suppliers and any inter-mediaries? For Sinaloa, reliance on secrecy, loyalty, fear, and payments in cash; for a coffee firm, credit transactions and legal/commercial understandings. Sinaloa must find substitutes for obtaining credit from banks and for relying on enforcement powers of courts. The CC can rely on both.
3. Who are the ultimate customers or consumers?
    a. For Sinaloa largely addicts; ordinary citizens for the CC.
    b. What is the nature of the relationship with them? The CC may use supermarkets and advertising to generate a very large consumer base; Sinaloa may sell to a relatively small addicted population through other users or street dealers.
    c. Is the relationship brokered by intermediary "wholesalers" or retail outlets? Sinaloa chooses to rely on street gangs for relationships with consumers of its drugs. Starbucks also has its own outlets.

36 Chapter 5

4. What are the potential substitutes for the product or services the organization is selling?
   a. Sinaloa has to think of how prescription painkillers like Vicodin may displace parts of its major business in heroin.
   b. Who is most likely to furnish those substitutes and how? A rival cartel in the case of Sinaloa vs. a rival chain of coffee shops like Dunkin' Donuts for the CC.
   c. What new lines of business might the organization itself like to add to its own product line? For Sinaloa, perhaps enriched forms of heroin.
5. What are the costs and difficulties of new entries into the market?
   a. For Sinaloa the question is: how can it overcome by fear or lethal force those that block its way to new markets; and
   b. How can it then create new and effective barriers to the entry of new competitors?
   c. For the CC it is the quality of the product plus the barriers to entry fortified by advertising.
6. What forms of geographic spread or product diversification of the business should the organization consider?
   a. How big will the European market be for cocaine?
   b. Should Sinaloa be considering marketing ecstasy?
   c. Starbucks has outlets worldwide.
7. What is the relationship to local and national government authorities for each business? How can government be made more supportive and less hostile?
   a. For the CC, lobbying, public relations, and campaign contributions.
   b. For the OCG, the same plus corruption and fear.
8. What culture must be developed for an effective organization?
   a. For Sinaloa a culture of secrecy, loyalty, and fear is central.
   b. For the CC an opposite culture may work better.

A business strategy very different from that of legitimate business also creates a pattern useful for identifying and locating organized crime. It emerges from consequences of having very different answers to these eight or more critical questions.

PART TWO
Law Enforcement on Steroids

Introduction

Part Two explores the U.S. answer to the dangers of organized crime. It begins by indicating why ordinary law enforcement by state or municipal police forces could not successfully eliminate organized crime. This led to a set of changes that we will examine carefully for four reasons.

First, the U.S. effort was successful in defeating the powerful and widespread Sicilian mafia in the United States. It may be successful elsewhere and certainly should be examined as a model for change.

Second, U.S. law enforcement relied on changes in three quite specific areas: statutes defining crimes; authorization of new investigative techniques; and reorganized, centralized strategic responsibility to address the problems posed by organized crime. There is an important lesson here, too.

Third, the United States could not have been successful without certain preconditions, especially a broad public and political demand for a non-corrupt, determined, and skillful law enforcement to fight organized crime. Satisfying this precondition of the other changes may be the hardest part of the program.

Fourth, nothing is free. The changes may risk encouraging corruption as our discussion of the Whitey Bulger case illustrates.

The United States added new administrative structures and reallocated responsibility for law enforcement in this area from corruptible urban police to the better trained, more respected, far less corruptible federal level, and the FBI. It also developed, with the support of the courts and the legislature, new and powerful investigative techniques such as electronic surveillance, the use of informants, undercover operations, and witness protection.

Finally, the United States developed and enacted powerful new criminal statutes designed to deal with large organizations and the types of crimes they commit.

The Racketeer Influenced and Corrupt Organizations Act (RICO) increased the penalties for organized criminal activity, authorized new remedies, and allowed the simultaneous trial of the many activities of a sizable organization in a single forum. New money laundering statutes dealt with the proceeds of the businesses of organized crime and the facilitators of those businesses.

38 Part II

Still, it is important to recognize that the remarkable success of the United States in addressing the threat of La Cosa Nostra (LCN) was not wholly attributable to its strategies. The world was changing in a way that made the businesses of organized crime in the United States much less profitable and the participants more difficult to recruit.

These changes also required a new way of thinking about who should be doing what in these investigations. Part Two continues with a description of the many differences in the way a prosecutor thinks about an organized crime case compared to an "ordinary" murder, rape, or robbery.

The changes in U.S. law enforcement, the advantages and the dangers, are made more concrete and placed in a richer context by Chapter 9, a detailed account of what Boston's organized crime boss, Whitey Bulger, confronted when he was released from prison to find that there was a whole new structure of law enforcement in place, and how he exploited that new structure.

6

THE MECHANISMS AND DIFFICULTIES OF TRADITIONAL LAW ENFORCEMENT IN ADDRESSING ORGANIZED CRIME

The Familiar Goals of Prosecution Are Not Well Suited for Organized Crime

The ways in which criminal punishment is intended to make life better for civilized societies have been thoroughly explored over the last centuries. State-imposed retribution, substituting for private revenge, channels a powerful human motivation and seems to even out the score of good vs. evil replacing tit-for-tat violence. Criminal punishment also puts a stamp of social condemnation on certain behavior and makes clear that citizens are not disadvantaged for being law-abiding. Most of us fear the disruption of valued relationships that social condemnation brings. Punishment deters the individual defendant from repeating the crime and it deters people like him or her from attempting a similar crime. It incapacitates the individual for the period of a prison sentence. Possibly, punishment can also be used as a way of rehabilitating an individual. Punishment, like well-designed policing, can reduce the costs of public fear leading to excessively cautious behavior.

Now consider an organized crime group using local gangs to sell contraband, like drugs. There is little demand for retribution for crimes involving consensual conduct by the "victim." There may, in unusual situations, be a dangerous demand for revenge by an addict's family or friends, but this is surely rare and would be directed at the gang, not its supplier. Indeed, social condemnation is hardly present in sizable parts of the community that the dealer shares with the user. Incapacitation of one or several members of an organized crime group does not prevent the same number of similar crimes from occurring in the future. Indeed, it is likely to limit the occupational possibilities for the defendant after release to those provided by the organized crime group itself. Deterrence works for the sale of contraband but, as we have seen, the rewards for the unskilled are generally seen as greater in organized crime than elsewhere. The activity is dangerous but the potential rewards outweigh the danger for the young "soldiers" of drug cartels.

40 Chapter 6

Crimes Most Often Committed by Organized Criminal Groups—The Sale of Contraband, Public Corruption and Extortion—Leave Fewer Traces and Less Willing Witnesses of Their Criminal Activities

Let us assume at the moment that the tendency of a conviction to reduce crime were as great for organized criminal activity as for more ordinary street crime or white-collar crime. In a number of ways, a conviction is far less certain and more difficult. Compare two crimes: an organized criminal group's sale of drugs, and a robbery.

As an example of a robbery, consider the history of an actual one and compare it to drug sales. Imagine you were appointed the defense attorney for John Allen, who together with his best friend, Yogi, robbed a liquor store in Washington DC. The first requirement for the use of law enforcement to obtain a conviction and punishment (for the purposes we have described) is that the police know that a crime has been committed. The liquor store owner and his employee naturally and promptly reported the crime to the police. Now consider the drug sale. The purchaser of drugs or other forms of contraband gives no such notice. In a drug sale, there is often no one to play the critical role of the complainant, unless some form of assault accompanies the sale and that is hardly good for business.

Knowledge of the crime triggers an effort to identify a few likely suspects. A criminal investigation tries to match a collection of traces left by a criminal event, including memories and physical evidence, to traces left in a myriad of ways by a few suspects going about their daily lives. As the fit between the two collections of traces becomes close the investigation develops a suspect, but there is a "catch": collecting the traces of the lives of even a hundred, let alone one thousand, people during the period of the crime would be far too costly to be plausible as a form of investigation. Two questions—who had the motivation for the crime and who had the capacity and the opportunity to commit it—allow the investigators to develop a shortlist of suspects, the traces of whose lives around the time and place of the crime can be compared with the traces of the crime itself.

Generally, robbery is a crime that leaves too many motivated suspects and too large an unidentified group of those who might have had the opportunity and skills needed—making it a difficult crime to solve. But in the case of John and Yogi, they were seen leaving the liquor store and were followed, making them the suspects who had by far the best opportunity to commit the crime and thereby greatly narrowing the field of possible suspects. In contrast, a consensual crime, like drug trafficking or dealing, takes place in a location carefully chosen to be private (hiding from outside observation those who have access and opportunity to commit the crime) and involves financial motivations on the selling side. Thus, the category of opportunity doesn't narrow suspects, nor does the category of motivation.

With limited suspects, an ordinary investigation continues by gathering additional traces of the history of the individuals in the now-narrowed class of suspects and matching them with information from the crime scene or from witnesses to the event, including the complainant. In the case of John and Yogi, the car in which they fled was followed and later examined by the police. It contained disguises, guns, and money—all easily identifiable with the items seen and used at the crime scene at the liquor store. The source of many of these traces of the crime itself was the memories of the victims: the liquor store owner and his employee, who recalled what had happened to them—memories promptly recorded by the police. Both were anxious to convey this help to the police who were themselves motivated to solve the crime. But in the case of organized crime, there is generally an effort to corrupt the police and intimidate such witnesses—thus matching the two sets of traces becomes far more difficult.

In short, the probability of successfully solving a crime is initially a function of four factors, all of which make investigating the sale of contraband by an organized crime group relatively unlikely to be a success story. The factors determining the probability of success are: (1) the traces that are left by a particular crime and its perpetrator; (2) the willingness of private individuals to call these traces to the attention of the police; (3) the investigative resources (time, money, equipment, and enthusiasm) devoted by officials to the particular crime and the intelligence with which the resources are used; and (4) the activities that the police are permitted to engage in (or engage in illegally) while using these resources. Until the late 1960s in the United States and currently in Mexico these variables make the chance of success of the organized criminal group far greater than the chance of an unorganized pair of robbers.

The Traditional Mechanisms of Presenting Evidence to a Neutral Fact-Finder Are Actively Undermined by Organized Criminal Groups

Once an arrest is made, the evidence collected against the suspects must be presented to a neutral fact-finder if law enforcement and criminal justice are to be the vehicle for reducing a type of crime. In the case of John and Yogi, this was entirely straightforward. The judge felt physically secure and was extremely unlikely to be corruptible or corrupted. The same was true of the jury. The victims were cooperative and available. A prosecutor carefully argued the case that the traces of the suspects and the traces of the crime match so neatly that it could not be chance—that there was proof beyond a reasonable doubt.

In a prosecution of an organized crime group there is often an effort to bribe the judge or jury. Jimmy Hoffa was sent to jail for this. The victims and other witnesses may well be afraid to testify at trial. The only witnesses available are often "turned" criminals who have participated in illegal transactions themselves, making them subject to threats of long sentences unless they testify; and their testimony is far less credible with the jury. The crimes, instead of being specific, obviously harmful, and firmly located at a particular place and time, are likely to be systemic, have less clarity as to who are the victims, and are spread over a sustained period and a number of locations.

A single armed robbery would carry a heavy sentence for John and Yogi. In contrast, if all that can be shown under the rules of evidence is a single or a few voluntary transactions in contraband, the sentence is not likely to be severe. The threat of a severe sentence may gain the cooperation of guilty parties in the case of an armed robbery of a liquor store. The threat of a small sentence for one or two occasions of selling drugs, prostitution, gambling, or loan-sharking will not encourage criminal witnesses to take the grave risks of providing evidence for the prosecution against an organized and violent crime group.

Organized Crime Groups and the Law Enforcement Officers Investigating Them Compete in a Structured Way

Another way of making the same point is to note that the investigation and trial of an organized criminal activity is likely to involve not only the investigators capturing, and the prosecutors describing to a jury, the traces that can be found to match; it also involves a simultaneous contest with a group of suspects who have the capacity to conceal or destroy those traces before they can be found and used by law enforcement.

Ignoring, for the moment, the critically important protection of civil liberties under law, we can list the possible methods that police anywhere have available to detect the traces of a crime. There is only a

42 Chapter 6

limited set of steps that can be combined, in a more or less considered sequence, into a specific investigative plan. These include:

(1) Interview willing witnesses or seek to have unwilling witnesses testify under legal compulsion.
(2) Question the suspect under more or less coercive conditions.
(3) View and analyze publicly available physical evidence or use legal authority to search in private places.
(4) Review publicly available or voluntarily produced records or seek to have other records produced under legal compulsion.
(5) Engage in physical or electronic surveillance of the suspect's activities.
(6) Develop informants or offer rewards.
(7) Use undercover operations.

This list would be about the same in any political system, because legal and administrative limitations are not included in the analysis. The organized crime group has unusually effective means to counter many of these and is motivated and organized to use those means energetically. The contest has a certain structure. There is a set of rules that describe and limit permissible investigative behavior by the prosecution. Not all the seven categories of steps above are available to the prosecution in all situations. In particular, to protect the privacy of citizens, the more intrusive investigative steps—like a search, arrest, or electronic surveillance—require some basis in fact, usually certified by a judge, for believing that evidence will be found (or that the arrested person had committed a crime). Other steps, like physical surveillance from public places, do not require any such predicate ("probable cause" or "reasonable suspicion" or something else). The latter category—steps permissible without any predicate—must be taken first in order to develop the necessary predicate for the more intrusive steps, such as searching a house.

No less important, because of the likely determination of the suspect and the suspect's organization both to avoid continuing to produce new evidence during the investigation and to prevent law enforcement from finding prior traces that the suspect has produced and left where they can be discovered, the government will, as we will describe in Chapter 7, want to use investigative steps that are secret from the suspect, delaying for as long as possible the suspect's discovery that he is under investigation. Steps 5, 6, and 7 are examples of "covert" investigative steps. Overt steps like those in measures 1 through 4 are likely to alert the suspect to the need to avoid creating new traces (by, for example, discussions on the telephone) and to destroy physical evidence or discourage human testimony. The prosecution must therefore use covert steps before overt ones. The organized crime group will very much want corrupt law enforcement officers to alert them to such covert investigations.

In the end, if law enforcement is using only traditional, overt investigative steps, prosecuting only for very familiar historic crimes, and accepting the risk of corruption of the police or city government, honest law enforcement officers are likely to find themselves unable to develop cases against organized crime and consequently unenthusiastic about trying. These advantages of organized crime must be recognized, addressed, and countered, much as the United States did a half-century ago.

7

CREATING A LAW ENFORCEMENT CAPACITY TO ADDRESS THE ADVANTAGES OF ORGANIZED CRIME

The difficulties we have described in investigating an organized crime group such as La Cosa Nostra can be integrated into a single picture. Conducting an effective investigation of the ongoing activities of an organized crime group is characteristically different from solving a more ordinary, past crime. From the outset, organized crimes often go unreported. Organized criminal activity remains invisible either because all parties are willing participants in the crime—such as in drug sales, illegal gambling and police corruption—or because the victim and his family are afraid to report the crime—such as when a neighborhood business is extorted for "protection." As a result, the information which leads to the initiation of an organized crime investigation is often rumor in the form of second and third-hand reports of paid informants and defendants seeking to have their own criminal charges or sentences reduced. Prosecutors, police and jurors are skeptical of such self-serving information, particularly when it is ambiguous, conflicting, and not readily corroborated.

The differences continue after an investigation has been initiated. The police investigation of an isolated crime, such as a murder, is reactive. The police aren't trying to shut down a dangerous business; they are trying to determine who caused a death, with what level of choice or culpability, and why. And the investigation to address these questions is overt from the instant police cars respond to the scene of the killing. Everyone knows the police are conducting the murder investigation: police cars with flashing lights surround the area; policemen are walking up and down the streets, questioning witnesses. Prosecutors have little role in such a familiar type of investigation until the police arrest a suspect.

In contrast, an organized crime investigation is necessarily forward-looking, an effort to close down the business of a related set of individuals conducting an ongoing set of related lucrative crimes. The investigation is initiated because of informant information about crimes committed by members of a group in the past. But even if that information were not generally too fragmentary, conflicting and unverifiable to support a successful prosecution, the objective includes stopping the business to prevent ongoing crimes. Rather than working toward bringing an individual to justice for a crime he has committed in the past, the goal of an organized crime investigation is to look for evidence of an illegal business's crimes as they

44 Chapter 7

are being committed. This requires investigative techniques such as electronic surveillance, informants, and undercover agents that are typically not used when investigating isolated crimes.

An organized crime investigation is not focused on a single suspect, but on an organization whose reach, structure, longevity, resilience, and consequent danger substantially exceeds that of any single individual. The investigation's goal is to shut down some essential part of that organization, perhaps its leadership. Using everything legal in the law enforcement arsenal, prosecutors and law enforcement officers must be part of an integrated team from the outset of an organized crime investigation. The law requires the prosecutor to control certain investigative techniques (e.g., the grand jury) and to closely monitor the legality of how the police use others (e.g., physical and electronic searches). It requires the prosecutor to be attentive both to whether evidence might be suppressed because it was obtained illegally, and to whether the jury will be permitted to consider it under statutory and common law rules of evidence and privilege.

Prior to 1960, none of these procedures or investigative techniques for investigating organized crime existed. Organized crime was not distinguished as different from ordinary isolated crimes. Dealing with organized crime in the United States required a new law enforcement approach.

The impetus for this new way of addressing and combating organized crime was a tidal change in public attitudes. Starting with Senate hearings, led by Senator Estes Kefauver in 1950 and 1951, and built upon by Attorney General Robert Kennedy from 1955 to 1965, organized crime became viewed as a highly significant national threat. The result was to increase support for, and the prestige of, law enforcement personnel devoted to fighting organized crime with consequent growth in funding and authority.

For two decades beginning in the 1960s, the United States transformed its capacity to address organized crime so as to eliminate many of the advantages organized crime had enjoyed. The changes covered the investigating structures that would pursue organized crime cases, the investigative powers these new structures would enjoy, and the statutes they would have available to them. Let us consider these one at a time.

Reallocating Responsibility and Building New Organizational Structures

In the United States prior to 1960, the capacity to corrupt local law enforcement or the city government was a major advantage of organized crime. Covert investigative techniques would not remain covert. The prolonged and determined investigations that are required for combating organized crime could not take place.

A large part of this problem was solved by reallocating responsibilities between local police and the Federal Bureau of Investigation (FBI). Organized crime groups had infiltrated and corrupted local police in Chicago, New York, Las Vegas, New Orleans, Boston, and elsewhere. Transferring responsibility for the investigation of organized crime from local police to the Washington-based FBI cut local ties that had proved extremely advantageous to La Cosa Nostra. That alone would not have been successful unless the investigative agency at the federal level was itself substantially free from corruption, and also skilled, proud, and determined. The FBI largely satisfied these requirements.

There had been a second advantage to moving investigation and prosecution—for they had to work closely together—to the federal level. The new statutes and new investigative techniques that the FBI would be exploring could benefit greatly from the constant support of federal prosecutors (including the check that they exercised and the trust they created in the handling of new intrusive investigative techniques). Legally, the powers to obtain warrants and to compel testimony at a grand jury were vested in prosecutors. So Attorney General Robert Kennedy began to develop "organized crime strike forces" in which federal prosecutors and investigators worked closely together in investigations throughout the country—in places where organized crime may have developed a hold on a community or local government. The work of these federal teams benefited from a sharp focus of attention, immense public support, and growing expertise.

As we have seen in prior chapters, intimidation of witnesses was often crucial to organized crime's immunity to prosecution. Taking extremely seriously investigation and prosecution of intimidation as an obstruction of justice was only a first step in addressing such efforts. A separate structure in the Office of the United States Marshals was established during this period to operate a witness protection program that could significantly weaken the effects of intimidation on prosecution testimony. The program is expensive and difficult to operate safely, but it has been almost flawless in protecting the lives of those willing to endure the hardship of a change of identity and an isolating relocation. As we shall see, a third and even more effective response to intimidation was created by the statutory authorization of warrants for electronic surveillance combined with judicial acceptance that demonstrating probable cause for such a warrant did not require revealing the name of the individual providing that information to law enforcement.

Newly Available Investigative Techniques and Targets

Even skilled, energetic, and honest investigators needed to develop more effective techniques for covert investigations in order to successfully investigate a well-organized crime group. The new organized crime strike forces began to actively develop a broader understanding of the players and businesses of organized crime in the cities for which they were responsible. The gathering of criminal intelligence was essential for attacking a whole organization and its businesses. Because the activities of organized crime, like those of other businesses, are known to a group of people with whom the business deals (such as customers, suppliers, retailers, competitors, employees, or associates), they proved to be discoverable through the use of street informants, "turned" criminal defendants, and disgruntled "customers."

New statutes authorizing electronic surveillance opened up new avenues of investigation, at the same time as they helped to address the fears of witnesses and complainants. Phone taps or room bugs could, by the end of the 1960s, often be substituted at trial for the testimony of a frightened witness. Electronic surveillance of phones or searches of physical spaces required a predicate of "probable cause," but investigators could first gather evidence by steps that could be taken without any basis and only then turn to steps that required a predicate. Informants or government undercover agents placed secretly within the organization could provide the needed predicate, because neither the use of informants nor the use of undercover agents was considered a search by the Supreme Court and thus did not require any prior showing of reason to believe that evidence would be discovered.

Informants could and did also provide their own testimony against organized crime. The skepticism that juries felt about informants who had received major benefits in terms of reduced sentences or money could be remedied by having the informant wear a microphone or recording device to back up his testimony. An additional benefit of recording the interactions was that the informants would not have to subject themselves to the personal dangers of testifying at trial.

New Substantive Statutes

The final requirement for successfully battling organized crime was a new set of substantive statutes. A sizable organized crime group engages in a variety of criminal activities over a sustained period of time and in different locations. Each of those crimes may be minor, not creating the potential for a threat of punishment of lower level participants that is grave enough to justify the risk of cooperating against organized crime. Moreover, the traditional picture presented to a jury would be, at best, of a few separate minor crimes rather than something far more serious: knowing participation in a dangerous organized enterprise. The RICO (Racketeer Influenced and Corrupt Organizations Act) corrected these flaws by extending the variety and time period of acts and perpetrators that could be tried in the same prosecution and thereby providing a far fuller picture of collective illegality than even prior conspiracy law allowed. And it provided a new remedy of criminal forfeiture of the proceeds of the criminal enterprise (adding to other civil forfeiture statutes). One of the new investigative tools—uncovering financial transactions—could provide extremely valuable evidence as well as an opportunity for asset forfeiture. To avoid these consequences the organized crime group would seek to disguise the proceeds of crime as legitimate receipts of some form. Money laundering statutes criminalized that effort with severe sentences. At the same time these statutes put otherwise legitimate organizations in harm's way if they facilitated money laundering, a step that makes handling its money far more difficult for organized crime by motivating financial institutions to become allies of law enforcement.

A Word of Caution

We have argued that new and effective structures, powerful investigative tools, broad criminal statutes, and attention to the risks of corruption and intimidation are necessary to fight organized crime. But they may not be sufficient to deal with organized crime as it has appeared in Mexico, Colombia, Russia, and South Africa. In a remarkable chapter of his book, "Convictions." John Kroger, now President of Reed College but formerly a prosecutor in the Southern District of New York and Attorney General of Oregon, argues that while this set of statutes, structures, and investigative powers was useful to prosecute organized crime, other changes were occurring in the United States that severely weakened the LCN.

Kroger describes the four major activities of the LCN and the change in the environment in which these activities were to be carried out. First, illegal gambling was unable to compete with state lotteries and legal gambling establishments as these came into being during the federal government's attack on the LCN. Second, the drugs the LCN controlled from Sicily were replaced by drugs from Latin America, leaving the LCN without that monopoly. Third, loan-sharking to those with very poor credit ratings was rendered almost unnecessary by a mammoth increase in credit availability, particularly in the form of credit cards, in the United States. And finally, labor racketeering, a mainstay of extortion by the LCN, became far less profitable as union membership and power declined sharply in the United States.

Add to these economic changes (occurring at the same time as a determined law enforcement attack on the LCN), the fact that criminal organizations, like other organized crime groups elsewhere, had benefited immensely from the support of ethnic, local, or other social groupings—support which was once based for the LCN on discrimination against Italians. As the problem of discrimination declined and the prospects for Italian families improved, the community had little reason to support organized crime.

The combination was almost a "perfect storm" of difficulties for U.S. organized crime. So, Kroger argues, one should be cautious in concluding too confidently that, if the requirements of law enforcement effectiveness are vigorously and intelligently pursued, organized crime will be as battered in other countries as the LCN was in the United States.

Still, even with all these changes the last necessary step was for prosecutors and enforcement agents to learn how best to use these new tools to maximize their effectiveness—the subject of the next chapter.

8

NEW STRATEGIES FOR PROSECUTORS OF ORGANIZED CRIME

Some part of almost every sizable ethnic group in the United States has, at some time, engaged in organized crime. The fictional investigation we are about to describe involves a Chinese-American group. It could as easily have had the ethnicity of any other segment of our population.

As we take you through the investigation of a hypothetical organized crime group, you will see three recurrent qualities. First, the investigation is conducted by an integrated team of investigators and prosecutors. This core of specialized investigators and prosecutors must then expand and work through a sometimes untrustworthy group of alliances if it is to develop the evidence it needs. Second, the investigation develops in a characteristic pattern: using less intrusive techniques before more intrusive ones; moving from a covert phase to an overt one; and considering larger pools of potential subjects before narrowing to target individuals. Third, the investigation is carefully planned rather than reactive, thoughtfully integrating and sequencing investigative techniques all the way up to and through the charging phase itself.

The Investigation Begins

As a prosecutor in a U.S. Attorney's office in a mid-sized city, you are visited by a local FBI agent, Agent Terri Monaco. She advises you that she works frequently in the Chinatown area of your city and has been hearing, from an informant, that there is a gambling den at 11 Shanghai Street. The informant says it runs every night with local restaurant and small business employees as the primary customers during weeknights and high stakes players moving in on Friday and Saturday nights. Agent Monaco tells you that she has checked telephone company records which show a phone on the 2nd floor in the name of The Asian Trading Company. She has come to you at this early stage because she wants authorization to install a pen register and trap-and-trace device on that phone.

In most cases street crime prosecutors do not see a case file until they are in the courtroom. With ordinary street crimes police investigate; prosecutors prosecute. However, in a federal organized crime case, law enforcement agents and prosecutors are driven together early in the investigation both by the legal framework and by the need to share well-learned investigative "best practices."

The laws and Constitution of the United States sharply limit both the agents' ability to compel witnesses to provide information and the agents' access to more intrusive investigative surveillance techniques without judicial sanction that must be sought by prosecutors. Thus, unless agents collaborate with their prosecutorial counterparts, they are severely limited in the investigative techniques they can use. They can question witnesses and, broadly speaking, look, see and hear only those things which everyday citizens can. Thus, agents can sit in a restaurant hoping to overhear bits and pieces of a conversation at an adjacent table but, without a court order, cannot conceal recording equipment at the table. They can question a witness whom they believe may have information, but, without invoking the power of the court, cannot compel that witness to give them answers to questions. Consequently, the need of organized crime agents to use these intrusive and compulsory investigative techniques drives them into collaboration with their prosecutorial counterparts early in a case. In our case, Agent Monaco sought to work with the prosecutor's office early in her investigation so that she could obtain a judicial order for a pen register and trap-and-trace device, one which would authorize her to learn in real time the numbers being called from, and the numbers calling into, a particular telephone.

Jointly conducted organized crime investigations are not merely forced marriages, however. They are the product of 50 years' experience in best practices. Agents bring unique assets to an investigation. Ideally, they are familiar with the community in which an investigation will take place, are familiar with the backgrounds and suspected activities of some members of the criminal organizations operating there, have an informant base, and are experienced questioners. Prosecutors, especially experienced ones, may bring a number of these assets as well. After years of investigating organized crime, they also have institutional knowledge and skills in how to use techniques available only to the prosecutors, such as using a grand jury to question witnesses.

It is important that prosecutors view evidence collection from a critically different perspective. Prosecutors from the outset are concerned with evidence at trial. Engaged prosecutors ensure that intrusive and compulsory investigative techniques are used lawfully, and thus that the evidence they collect is admissible at trial. They also consider whether facts are obtained second- or third-hand (and thus may be inadmissible as hearsay evidence), or have the direct impact and greater credibility of first-person observation. Finally, throughout the investigation, they will try to ensure that the facts collected are sufficient to meet their ultimate and difficult burden of proof—proof beyond a reasonable doubt—with respect to the members of the organization and their alleged crimes. And the facts that must be proved to convict under new statutes like RICO are not always obvious to agents.

Agent Monaco has come to you, seeking to add to her informant's information the telephone numbers of potential associates. Investigations typically, though not always, lay groundwork with less intrusive techniques and only then move toward more intrusive ones. As a matter of law, more intrusive steps frequently require a factual predicate that only emerges as other less intrusive steps are taken. Moreover, intrusive ones can be both financially and politically costly. They are best used when one has already obtained as much information as possible elsewhere. Based on your experience, you discuss with Agent Monaco other, less intrusive, options for obtaining background information, perhaps asking:

1. Do the agencies' files contain any other reports about activities at 11 Shanghai Street?
2. Are there any local police reports about activities at 11 Shanghai Street?
3. What do public records show about the ownership and business activities of The Asian Trading Company?

50 Chapter 8

4. What can you learn about who is receiving mail at 11 Shanghai Street by using a mail cover—looking at the return address of envelopes delivered to that address?
5. What is contained in the trash left outside of 11 Shanghai Street? Are there things that appear associated with a gambling den, or indicate who might be associated with it?
6. Should you put a video camera out on the public street to record who goes in and out of 11 Shanghai Street (and when), in the hope of later identifying them?

None of these techniques requires a court order in the federal criminal justice system. Each is considered less intrusive because it reveals only those things that are generally exposed to the public by the individuals about whom you are seeking to collect information. However, the background information they might generate would inform a decision on whether to proceed with Agent Monaco's proposed investigation, potentially suggest other federal agencies or police departments that should be added to the investigative team, and begin to provide the predicate for more intrusive investigative techniques requiring judicial approval.

Agent Monaco has checked with a trusted friend in the local police department and found that the police department raided 11 Shanghai Street three times during the last 18 months. The returns from the search warrants show only small amounts of money being recovered, although a dozen or more people were arrested on each occasion. Those arrested were typically released after paying small fines.

In the meantime, you have checked with an agent you have worked with in the past in Immigration and Customs Enforcement (ICE). You have found that ICE has an informant who is a regular participant in games at 11 Shanghai Street. This informant confirms Agent Monaco's earlier information. He adds that, as in most gambling dens, loans are being made to losing bettors at extortionate rates.

The ICE agent describes their confidential informant (CI) as a 23-year-old Chinese man who is living in the United States. He has had two arrests for possession of cocaine. The proceeding for the second is still pending. Following his conviction on the first possession charge, ICE began deportation proceedings, which led to his offer to cooperate.

Back in your office, as lead prosecutor you must consider expanding the investigative team. ICE appears to have a witness with critical information, but they consider him "their" witness while your investigation is being run by another agency, the FBI. Competition between investigative agencies for funding, convictions, and press headlines often make them reluctant to share their agents and sources of information. This is a marriage you indeed may need to force.

More problematic is whether to bring in the local police department. They too may have valuable information for the organized crime investigation you are pursuing. Unlike the FBI, they have intimate knowledge of the streets they have been patrolling for months and perhaps years. They know the people who are going in and out of the gambling den, and they have participated in searches a number of times. During each of those searches, they have seen who has been present and what the activity has been.

It is troubling, though, that with so many searches so little money has been found on the tables. The police detectives with the most intimate knowledge of the organization's operation may also be pocketing its money. There is a risk that, if you bring them into your investigation, you will acquire not only critical street-level information but also a devastating source of leaks on your still-covert investigation.

The most effective investigative techniques are also the most covert and highly intrusive. Only while an investigation is covert can you watch and listen to the planning and attempted execution of crimes by a group's members, collecting detailed, first-hand evidence critical to successful organized crime prosecutions. But collection of this intimate level of information requires electronic eavesdropping or the introduction of law enforcement spies, widely feared techniques generally tolerated only to address threats of severe criminal activity, terrorism, or espionage.

You must decide at this point whether to negotiate a deal with ICE's CI to inform on the group's membership to learn about its ongoing criminal activities, and, eventually, to provide testimony at trial. Two overarching factors are in the balance. First, how do the crimes the CI has committed and now wants "forgiven" compare to those that you are investigating? The wise rule of thumb—often enforced by juries—is that the prosecutor should not offer a deal for information when the informer is more dangerous or guilty than the persons he implicates. If the CI is simply a drug user, his crimes are less weighty than if his possession of cocaine is indicative of his being a drug dealer. So, reducing his charge to catch a gambling ring might be warranted if he is a user but not if he is a dealer. Similarly, if the crime under investigation is gambling, the state's interest in obtaining the CI's testimony to produce a successful investigation is less compelling than if the crimes under investigation include extortion, corruption, and racketeering.

Second, what is the apparent trustworthiness of the CI? Is he going to become a double-agent? Can you trust what he says? Will a jury? If not, what can you do? As a prosecutor, you are looking for admissible and credible evidence that you can use to obtain court-authorized search warrants and electronic surveillance orders, and, ultimately, to offer at trial. With few exceptions, cooperators are also criminals and thus their credibility is inherently suspect. His statements to you may be self-serving lies. The cooperator may also be acting as a double-agent reporting to the organized crime group as well as to law enforcement.

You could introduce an undercover federal agent, bypassing the CI's potential weaknesses. An undercover agent will not tip off your investigation, will follow instructions, and will be credible at trial. However, in an insular community, particularly one in which a foreign language is spoken, introducing an outsider may be all but impossible. Another option is to record what the CI says and does while interacting with the gambling ring. In its simplest form, under federal law Agent Monaco can, without need of court approval, put a recording device on the person of the cooperator or on his telephone with his permission so that there is an unchallengeable record of each of his conversations with suspects.

After interviewing the confidential informant, Mr. Wong, you have agreed to ask ICE to postpone his deportation proceedings in exchange for his cooperation. He has been told you cannot guarantee what ICE will do, but that you will promise not to use what he tells you against him in any criminal proceedings.

Sometime later, using information obtained from Wong and other information gathered, you obtained a court order authorizing a room bug in the gambling den. The recordings are frequently inaudible due to the background noise; moreover, the agents are unable in most cases to identify who is speaking. But what you do hear confirms that gambling is going on, sometimes with high stakes.

Wong tells you that the manager of the den, Sung, cannot himself approve high stakes games or any major loan to a bettor. The manager has to call the gang leader, who is rarely present himself. Wong does not know who the gang leader is.

At this point in the investigation, information has emerged that is adequate to raise suspicions of loan-sharking, conspiracy, and public corruption in addition to gambling. However, the investigative team is not clear about who is involved in the most serious crimes. You have information about the low-level people, the people working in the gambling den. But you do not know who is authorizing the extortionate loans and who in the police department, if anyone, is taking bribes.

You also do not know whether this is the only business location of the organization, or one of many. If it is one of many, you do not know who is participating in the other businesses.

52 Chapter 8

At this point, as prosecutor you must make three strategic decisions:

(1) Which of the suspects do you plan to prosecute and which do you instead hope to turn into witnesses?
(2) What potential crimes do you intend to pursue? For example, should public corruption be included?
(3) At what point is it worth sacrificing the advantages of secrecy to gain the use of some powerful overt investigative techniques, such as court-authorized search warrants and compelled testimony before a grand jury?

The first two decisions are related in an important way. Their answers are needed to focus the investigation going forward. Focus is necessary to concentrate investigative resources on the most promising and important suspects and crimes. But it requires walking away from some individuals and from some crimes—both to maximize the effectiveness of use of investigative resources on other people and crimes and also for increased certainty that whoever is to be prosecuted is in fact—and will be found—guilty. The heart of the matter is that successful organized crime cases cannot be made without at some point directing the full focus of investigators on particular individuals and crimes, in an effort to identify every piece of evidence with regard to each. What's more, a concentrated focus may be necessary to promptly gather the traces of a crime before organized criminals are able to cover them up.

The decision to focus an investigation becomes difficult because, if the investigators walk away too quickly from some individuals and some crimes, they may be giving a free pass to serious crimes. Walking away also involves sharply increasing the attention on the suspects and crimes that remain, with real costs to the reliability of fact-gathering. An early focus creates the risks caused by over-enthusiasm at too early a stage: ignoring evidence of the innocence of focal suspects or the guilt of others; and concluding that ambiguous evidence against one of the remaining suspects in one of the remaining crimes is more probative than it might otherwise seem.

As an example of the last, the fact that one particular police detective was involved in the search of the gambling den on each of the occasions of prior investigation of the gambling could be evidence that he is protecting the gambling den, but it might be merely a scheduling coincidence. Similarly, the fact that he appears on Agent Monaco's trap-and-trace record as having phoned the gambling organization may reflect his involvement or that he has been working to develop an informant base within the community. Investigators moving too quickly from large groups of suspects to individuals have led to notorious embarrassments costly to the reputation of the investigating agency, such as those suffered by the FBI in its botched investigations of the bombing at the Atlanta Olympics and of the possible theft of secrets at the Los Alamos Laboratory.

Your investigation critically still remains covert at this stage. As we have described, in a robbery or murder investigation, all investigative activities are overt from the outset. For example, a murder victim's violent boyfriend knows that he is under investigation for the murder and there is little to be gained by police concealing any investigative activities he would anticipate. In contrast, an organized crime group secretly committing victimless crimes is likely to be unaware for some time that it has been identified and is under investigation. So, with an organized crime investigation, investigative activities often begin covertly. There is a tactical advantage to be gained by prosecutors and agents when they have not used investigative techniques revealing to those under investigation the existence of the investigation. Employing electronic surveillance equipment, such as the bug that has been secreted in the gambling den, can be an extraordinarily powerful and effective technique in establishing a criminal organization's command

New Strategies for Prosecutors **53**

structure and implicating its leaders. However, it is rendered substantially ineffective once those speaking know they are being listened to.

The move from a covert investigation to an overt investigation can only take place once. Once the criminals know they are under investigation, the ability to gather useful information from a wiretap, an undercover agent or other covert investigative techniques is generally lost. The choice, therefore, as to when to move from covert investigative techniques to overt ones is a critically important tactical decision. In our gambling den example, investigators continue to use only covert investigative techniques. Certainly, you could bring gamblers before the grand jury and ask them questions. You could also bring the employees or even the den's manager before the grand jury. But the likelihood of their testimony being forthcoming is extremely low and you would have lost all the advantages of remaining covert.

Organized criminal groups are structured to provide insulation to their leaders; the higher the leader, the greater the insulation. The means the gambling den leader is using to insulate himself are also typical. He allows only the manager of the gambling den—no doubt a long-term and trusted associate—to communicate with him. He is never present when extortionate loans are extended or the gambling den, itself, is in operation. Those people who know his true identity are strictly limited. When he talks to those who do know him, almost certainly he talks in code and, perhaps, using prepaid, disposable cell phones. Successful investigations of organized criminal groups generally require the iterative and integrated use of investigative techniques to identify the group's leaders. Through the first rounds of the investigation, your investigative team has been able to identify the manager of the den, Sung. By focusing your investigative techniques on him, not as the primary suspect but rather as a source of information about others, it may now be possible to get closer to identifying the gang's leader.

The careful combination of investigative techniques can facilitate the identification of individuals and of critical evidence when individual techniques, used separately in the course of a traditional investigation, would not.

The electronic surveillance was extended to the manager's phone. Combining the use of a cooperating witness with electronic surveillance, you now ask Wong to lose money in the gambling den and to try to borrow money to continue to play. Wong's request for a loan triggers a call within minutes from Sung, the den's manager, to the group's unidentified leader for approval of the loan. Agent Monaco's pen register reveals the number Sung calls and you issue a grand jury subpoena for all records relating to that phone, taking you a step closer to identifying the group's leader.

From the records you learn that Sung called a man named Mao, who authorized a loan to Wong at 5 percent per week interest. On one prior occasion, Wong observed Hsu, an employee of a local restaurant, helping out at the gambling tables. Wong has learned that Hsu obtained an extortionate loan during a night of serious gambling losses. The loan remains unpaid. Scared, Hsu has been trying everything he can to work it off.

Wong is prepared to take the personal risk of testifying in open court but he wants his cocaine charges dismissed and lawful residency in the United States. When you debriefed him, you learned that he can testify both about the organization's current structure and about a brothel it is running across town. Wong says that only one of the employees of the gambling den works at the brothel as well. He is the "runner" Chang, who picks up cash from both places and delivers it to Mao.

You understand that few saints have worked in organized crime groups. If you and Agent Monaco are going to have witnesses available to testify at trial against the various members of the organized crime group, you are going to need to make a deal with Wong, Hsu, or Chang. The trade-offs which must be made in this decision are common in an organized crime case. Wong, the CI, is the one with the deepest knowledge of the organization. He is trusted by the criminal organizations because of his own extensive criminal activity. You as the prosecutor will need to dismiss drug charges against him to obtain his

54 Chapter 8

testimony, a step that the defense counsel for Mao will remind the jury repeatedly. The jury will be deeply skeptical of anything said by an illegal alien who benefits so extensively from his involvement in the case. He may, they think, simply be saying what he believes the government wants to hear.

Hsu, the gambler, doesn't come with this baggage but appears to know significantly less about the group. To the jury, he may appear sympathetic as someone who simply got in over his head. However, he may be unwilling to testify, not because he is a bad citizen but because of the toll it will take on his family if he does. He lives with his family in a culturally, linguistically, and physically insular community. If he testifies, or even if it becomes known that he is considering testifying, his family may be threatened or harmed by members of the organized criminal group to prevent or punish his testimony.

Finally, there is the runner, Chang. Wong could be encouraged to testify by the promise of remaining in the United States and having criminal charges against him dropped. Hsu, if he could be convinced, could be lured to testify against the organization with the promise that he would be freed from his extortionate debt to the organization and protection would be provided to him as a witness. What remains to "encourage" Chang's testimony? He is a critical bridge between two of the organization's criminal activities, the gambling den and the brothel.

As the prosecutor, you have the power to bring heavy charges against Chang. Although a low-level employee of the organized criminal group, he has participated in two predicate crimes in furtherance of the enterprise. He has thus become guilty under the RICO statute. While bringing a racketeering charge against Chang may seem disproportionate to the low-level activities in which he participated, only that threat may be sufficient to induce him to cooperate and testify in this important investigation. Within the United States, drug charges with lengthy minimum mandatory sentences are frequently brought against low-level drug organization employees to obtain precisely this kind of testimony.

If you bring heavy charges against Chang and he testifies pursuant to a plea agreement, you can *then* ask for only a greatly reduced sentence or even dismiss the charges. As prosecutor, you have obtained critical evidence against a significant and potentially dangerous organization. If Chang does not agree to testify, however, one can legitimately ask whether you have justly used your discretion, or abused it, if you bring very serious charges against a quite modest player simply to establish the credibility of the threat Chang ignored in refusing to testify.

You have obtained search warrants for the gambling den and the gang leader's home. When agents search the gambling den, they find four very active tables, each of which has a dealer. The agents pat down each of the dealers to ensure the safety of those executing the warrant and find that one of the dealers has a semi-automatic pistol with an effaced serial number. Agents arrest that dealer, photograph the interior of the operation, identify all of those present, and seize $15,000 from the gambling tables.

Simultaneously, (and before spread of the word of the raid on the gambling den) agents search Mao's condominium where they find and seize bank records for The Asian Trading Company. These records reflect regular cash deposits ranging from $5,000 to $25,000. The agents also find a safety deposit key. The safe deposit box, later opened with a warrant, contains over $1 million in cash. Both the building in which the brothel operates and Mao's BMW were purchased with checks from The Asian Trading Company.

Often overlooked, the charging strategy is a final integral part of the investigation of an organized criminal group. There is often immense institutional pressure from supervisors and those at the investigating agencies, to prosecute a large, well-publicized case. Investigators have invested significant amounts of resources in the investigation and the returns for them are the accolades that would come with a big case. As a result, agency heads and the head of the prosecutor's office itself are likely to push for a racketeering indictment charging as many people as possible at once. But, besides being and appearing unfair to the minor participants, this may well leave you with fewer witnesses and less evidence against the organization's principals than you could obtain by employing a different, more tactical charging strategy.

With greater patience, you could first charge the dealer from whom agents seized the automatic pistol. Absent the government's acquiescence, a judge will be statutorily bound to sentence him to a long mandatory/minimum sentence following his near certain conviction. His cooperation and testimony are his only escape, providing you with evidence that you could use later in your broader racketeering case. You could also bring an initial round of prosecutions against those of the group's enforcers you have been able to identify. Taking them off the street first could encourage witnesses such as Hsu to come forward by reducing their fear of retribution.

9

A DOUBLE-EDGED SWORD

How Improved Law Enforcement Aided Whitey Bulger*

Beginning in 1961, a combination of sophisticated new techniques and innovative statutes enabled law enforcement to locate, target, and prosecute organized crime, leading to a great reduction of mob activity in both Chicago and New York by 1980. By contrast, Boston experienced the gradual expansion of several organized crime groups through the 1980s—not in spite of these legal developments, but often assisted by them.

Boston's descent into its most violent era of organized crime, which lasted from 1970 through the 1990s, resulted to a large extent from the complex relationship between Boston's most notorious criminal, James "Whitey" Bulger, and federal law enforcement. Beginning in the 1960s, Bulger rapidly ascended through the ranks of Boston's Irish mobs, and became one of the FBI's mostly closely guarded informants in 1974. Over the next twenty years, Bulger manipulated his handlers into providing him with an invaluable competitive edge: inside information that enabled him to locate and assassinate gang competitors and fellow informants, extort funds from local illicit operations as well as legitimate businesses, and consolidate a criminal network that extended over the entire city, all while enjoying immunity from investigation and prosecution.

We have seen in the previous chapters how the U.S. methods of empowering law enforcement to deal with even a powerful form of organized crime worked. Administrative changes created a centrally managed and focused program combining the responsibilities of a close-knit team of prosecutors and a group of FBI investigators. New statutes made it a serious crime to knowingly play even a minor role in a criminal enterprise. The result was a new level of pressure on even minor players to assist law enforcement. The new statute, RICO, also allowed the prosecutor to present to the jury a far fuller and more frightening picture of a criminal enterprise that has endured and spread its businesses into many new areas of illegal activity.

At the same time strong measures were taken to weaken the advantages organized crime enjoyed. Corruption and intimidation of witnesses were taken very seriously by the new and focused law enforcement units. Witness protection and the capacity to hide the name of informants in seeking a warrant made giving information much safer. The use of covert investigative technologies grew sharply with new legal powers to employ electronic surveillance, undercover FBI agents, and informants.

Not least important, the rewards of publicity, Congressional favor, and admiration of colleagues and higher ups shifted abruptly to the agents and prosecutors engaged in a battle with organized crime.

The Bulger case that follows illustrates the power of the new organizational structure, new criminal statutes, newly available investigative techniques, and the focus on a single organization, the LCN. It also illustrates the motivating influence of rewards of prestige for a prosecutor or agent working in this area. But the case plays a more important role as a reminder that concentrated, focused, secretive law enforcement power can be captured by its targets and turned into a weapon of a criminal enterprise. It can be used to hide crimes, to protect against prosecution, to disclose the use of covert investigative techniques by rival law enforcement agencies and to prevent their use against a target. In short, the very changes that made law enforcement effective against organized crime could, if carefully corrupted, make law enforcement itself the way to deal with the two greatest threats to a criminal enterprise: the danger of prosecution and the danger posed by rival organized crime groups.

For example, the secrecy that is necessary to protect informants from gang reprisals can also be used to hide the informant's unauthorized crimes from his supervisors. The exposure of a criminal gang to intelligence-based surveillance can also be used by an informant to target his business rivals. The focused attention needed to understand who is doing what and why in a criminal enterprise can be directed by a Whitey Bulger to free his own gang from law enforcement attention. The needed close cooperation of prosecutors and investigators can result in the prosecutor not supervising and not providing a check on what the investigators are doing.

As we shall see in the case that follows, each of the powers and strategies needed by law enforcement to investigate and prosecute a lasting multi-product criminal enterprise can be turned against law enforcement by a clever enough suspect who has either corrupted, or won the unquestioning trust of, an overconfident or overambitious, agent and prosecutor.

What follows recounts Bulger's role in the aggressive expansion of Irish gangs during the simultaneous erosion of the Italian mafia in Boston, and examines the law enforcement missteps that shielded Bulger from prosecution until he escaped the city in 1994, when his crimes became too obvious to ignore. It then examines the actions taken by law enforcement to finally dismantle Bulger's criminal network.

Early Crimes in a New Era

Bulger began his foray into crime in South Boston, or "Southie," a tightly knit neighborhood with a large working-class Irish population and a colorful history of political bosses and gang violence. His string of crimes, including theft and assault, made him familiar to the police by the time he reached his early teens, to the point where the Boston police gave him the nickname "Whitey" for his flash of blond hair. Among Southie residents he quickly earned a "Robin Hood" reputation that he would maintain until 1994, when the police finally linked Bulger to several murders.

Throughout his early criminal career, Bulger remained closely affiliated with Southie's fluid network of Irish street gangs.[1] In 1956, when Bulger was in his mid-twenties, he was arrested after a botched armed robbery attempt and sentenced to over twenty years in prison, but his sentence was eventually commuted to nine years and he was released in 1965. That incarceration—the only jail time Bulger would face for the next four decades—allowed him to narrowly escape the Boston gang wars that, according to a retired colonel from the Massachusetts State Police, might very well have ended the Bulger crime regime before it truly began.[2]

58   Chapter 9

New Tools Against Organized Crime, 1960–1970

By the time Bulger emerged from prison the Kefauver hearings of 1950–1951 and Attorney General Robert Kennedy's campaign against organized crime had drawn significant public and government interest.[3] The public's attention was especially captured when in 1963 the U.S. government launched a formal investigation into organized crime and for the first time in U.S. history heard testimony from a high-ranking member of the mafia: Joseph Valachi, a lieutenant in the Italian mob family La Cosa Nostra. One official tasked with organizing the investigation would later comment, "What [Valachi] did is beyond measure ... Valachi named names. He revealed what the structure was and how it operates. In brief, he showed us the face of the enemy."[4] The hearings immediately secured the Italian mafia a place in American consciousness, prompting lawmakers to pass legislation that would aid law enforcement to combat organized crime networks.[5]

Prior to this time, authorities had been severely handicapped in their efforts to investigate and prosecute organized crime. To be effective, investigations had to focus on a criminal organization rather than on individual crimes. Familiar avenues of evidence were too fragmentary and inadequate to meet the central challenge of any organized crime investigation: monitoring the present, rather than discovering the past, to identify the participants in a network of individuals engaged in an ongoing and interconnected series of crimes. Even by 1963, the very structure of each organized crime network continued to present a formidable challenge for prosecutors.

Additionally, local efforts to prosecute criminals remained haphazard, disorganized, and not strategically targeted. Corruption in local law enforcement, which had the primary responsibility for dealing with organized crime at the time, was widespread. Even if an investigation was launched, law enforcement lacked the tools to gather evidence or to convince lower-ranking mob members to cooperate in bringing even competing gangs down.

Three key developments would enable law enforcement to begin pursuing organized crime in earnest. In 1951 the Kefauver Committee,[6] in conjunction with the Senate and a later working group organized by the White House, began to urge the federal government to create a new organizational structure for combating organized crime: a federal "task force" of skilled and energetic investigators. The resulting specialized task forces represented an immediate attempt to reduce corruption and inefficiency.

After taking over the Department of Justice (DoJ) in 1961, Attorney General Robert Kennedy finally acted on this recommendation, expanding the DoJ's Organized Crime and Racketeering Section.[7] As early as 1965 Kennedy directed regional offices of the FBI to seek carefully vetted local assistance when investigating organized crime. Slowly, the U.S. government began to institutionalize these new investigative units—a practice that soon became systematized with the introduction of specialized federal–local organized crime task forces in a number of cities throughout the country.

However, investigators also required new techniques to conduct covert investigations against well-organized crime groups. This prompted the second key development: the authorization of new investigative techniques, including more advanced surveillance methods, new grounds for wiretapping, expanded protocols for finding and handling mob informants, and a witness protection program to limit mob retaliation.

Previously, two major investigative shortcomings had continued to trouble law enforcement. First, until the federal government began to lead local law enforcement, police departments in particular lacked the technology or the skills to perform the sophisticated surveillance that would produce substantive evidence. Second, while the so-called Valachi hearings had established the need to enlist informants as a central tenet of organized crime investigation, the threat of prosecution was too weak to coerce lower-ranking members of the mob into cooperating, while the threat of retaliation was strong enough to keep them silent.

But beginning in the 1960s—just as Bulger was released from prison—the government began to establish new surveillance techniques that would directly threaten mobsters. In 1968, the Omnibus Crime Control and Safe Streets Act first established government procedures for wiretapping. The act would authorize hundreds of mob wiretaps over the next decade.[8] Then, in 1970, the government created the Witness Protection Program which increased the flow of information from frightened witnesses.

Despite these two developments, prosecution of organized crime networks remained limited. The then-existing statutes left prosecutors unable to provide the full picture of acts and perpetrators to the juries they hoped would convict members of the mob. Then, in 1970, Congress passed the Racketeer Influenced and Corrupt Organizations Act (RICO), which made it a federal crime "punishable by up to twenty years in jail (and, in cases involving murder, life)" for a person "to commit two or more specific state or federal crimes as part of an 'enterprise'—an organized group—that affects interstate commerce."[9] After the passage of RICO, mob bosses could be prosecuted for crimes their associates had committed under their supervision, allowing law enforcement to build cases based on a variety of behaviors by different groups and their organizing superiors. After a series of court decisions clarified RICO's very broad reach, the statute became the centerpiece of law enforcement efforts to take down different strands of Boston's mob scene.

The federal government's new resources and tools dramatically increased the possibility of a successful and cohesive campaign against organized crime. But in the case of Whitey Bulger, they also exposed the government to new, unforeseen vulnerabilities: the possibility that a mob boss would become an FBI informant and use his relationship with the federal government to avoid investigation and prosecution while continuing his criminal activities. Each time an indictment was issued, a wiretapping attempt was made, or law enforcement or another mobster implicated Bulger or his gang, Bulger and his closest associates somehow avoided prosecution. This critical manipulation of the centerpiece of law enforcement's organized crime strategy permitted Bulger to escape prosecution for nearly four decades, while the majority of Boston's mob leaders were eventually indicted, arrested, and convicted.

The Irish Gang Wars: 1965–1972

Although Bulger returned to Boston in 1965, it took several years before he resumed his involvement with organized crime, specifically with Boston's loose network of fiercely competitive Irish gangs.[10] By 1965, power in Boston was divided between the well-organized Boston chapter of the Italian mafia (the all-too-familiar LCN) and three Irish gangs: the Mullens and the Killeens, both operating out of Southie, and the newly formed Winter Hill Gang, located across the Charles River in Somerville, a neighborhood just north of Harvard Square.[11] By 1971, the Mullens and the Killeens competed violently for control of Southie. Bulger initially allied with the Killeens as an enforcer, taking out several Mullens when the opportunity arose. In 1971, sensing an opportunity, Bulger turned on the Killeens and secretly made an offer to the boss of Somerville's Winter Hill Gang, Howie Winter: he would take out the Killeens in exchange for membership in Winter Hill and protection from the Killeens and the Mullens.

Shortly after Bulger's meeting with Winter, Donald Killeen, the leader of the Killeen gang and Bulger's former patron, was assassinated at his son's fourth birthday party. Sources dispute whether Bulger or the Mullens had committed the murder. Regardless, most accounts agree that shortly thereafter Bulger

60 Chapter 9

approached Donald Killeen's brother while he was jogging, pointed a gun at him, and said: "It's over. You're out of business. No more warnings." The Killeens ceded control of the gang and its loan-sharking operations to Bulger and disappeared quietly from the Boston gang scene. Bulger then partnered with Howie Winter to eliminate what remained of the Mullens. As former Massachusetts State Police Colonel Tom Foley describes, "[Winter and Bulger] went at the Mullens harder than the Killeens ever had. Whitey took out six of them in a two-day spree, and he'd slaughtered a full dozen by 1975." When he was done, Foley concludes, "the gang landscape had changed. Now there was Jerry Angiulo's Mafia operation [LCN] based in the North End, and Howie Winter's Winter Hill gang in Somerville, and that was pretty much it."

Taking Down La Cosa Nostra: 1975–1984

By 1975, just as the Irish gang wars concluded, and armed with a new organized crime squad and the antiracketeering RICO Act, the FBI in Boston began to target organized crime in earnest. Given the high-profile LCN arrests in New York during the 1950s and early 1960s, agents focused most of their attention on the Italian mafia. But even with the combination of savvy legislation and new investigative techniques—and especially in Boston, which was still recovering from the aftermath of the Irish gang wars—information about the different operating mobs remained largely fragmentary.

Starting in 1961, the FBI had encouraged its regional offices to cultivate informants to fill gaps in information about organized crime, explaining,

> Through well-placed informants we must infiltrate organized crime groups to the same degree that we have been able to penetrate the Communist Party and other subversive organizations … we cannot relax even momentarily our efforts in combating the criminal underworld.

The letter continued by highlighting the importance of recent information:

> The foundation from which we forge our attack must be kept strong and fresh with a full flow of information from well-placed informants … All Agents … should be constantly alert for the development of new informants … who may be in a position to assist us.[12]

By the 1970s, the FBI spoke even more directly on the subject of informants. Upon assuming the position of FBI director in 1972, Clarence M. Kelley stated simply: "Without informants, we're nothing." Armed with the fledgling Witness Protection Program to protect informants and other witnesses, and the concrete threat of prosecution represented by RICO, the FBI could now make a convincing case for a member of organized crime to cooperate with the FBI.

At the same time, FBI regional offices tentatively began to collaborate more closely with local law enforcement. The arrangement was largely one-directional, since the FBI remained suspicious of local law enforcement's history of corruption. Regardless, many wiretaps required local assistance to execute, and often lower-ranking gang members could only be taken off the streets for violations that local police could enforce, such as breaking the speed limit or not paying parking tickets. Like the FBI, local and state police in Boston were alarmed by the growing number of unsolved murders that could be tentatively linked to the Irish and Italian mobs and were eager to eliminate major organized crime players from the city.[13]

Throughout the 1970s, the FBI in Boston placed the highest priority on its investigation of LCN, specifically the New England Patriarca family, which was headquartered in Providence but who also had significant illegal operations in Boston. The FBI contributed its resources to a regional strike force that cooperated with several federal and local agencies, including the Drug Enforcement Agency and local police departments. Its strategy centered on using wiretaps to eliminate different levels of LCN—like "cutting the head off a snake," as Foley would later describe it. Each operation targeted a particular rank within the LCN, slowly accumulating charges and witnesses that could later be leveled against LCN's boss in Boston, Jerry Angiulo.

The case against Angiulo would take years to prepare, but in the late 1970s, and mostly by luck, the FBI also stumbled upon a possible case against the Winter Hill Gang: a massive horse race-fixing operation that stretched across eight states and was generating $8 million in profits ($33.5 million by today's standards). By 1979, the case against Winter Hill was complete and Howie Winter, along with forty-nine associates, was arrested on race-fixing and other charges.[14] Given the FBI's broader focus on the entire race-fixing network (which had originated in New Jersey) and the Boston task force's continued focus on LCN, Winter Hill's stunning setback barely resembled a sideshow. Even though several contemporary accounts indicated that Winter Hill was more violent than LCN, Jeremiah O'Sullivan, the federal prosecutor who handled the case, treated Winter Hill's prosecution as a stepping stone toward the ultimate goal: the final case against the Italian mafia.[15] When Jerry Angiulo was finally led out of a North End restaurant in handcuffs in 1983, he promised to return before his pork chop dinner got cold. Instead, in 1984 he and his co-defendants were sentenced to 45 years in prison.

Boston in the 1980s: The End of the Mob, the Beginning of Organized Crime

The 1979 horse race-fixing case against Winter Hill, followed by the 1984 RICO indictment of Angiulo and dozens of LCN members, should have set Boston on the same trajectory as New York and Chicago: toward the inevitable decline of organized crime. But even the indictment of Winter Hill and the LCN did not seem to affect racketeering in Boston significantly. Loan-sharking and gambling continued, as did extensive narcotics operations.[16] Complaints of extortion continued to reach the FBI and local law enforcement. As the 1980s continued, police realized that another mobster had stepped into the vacuum left by Howie Winter and Jerry Angiulo: Whitey Bulger.

At first Bulger's evasion of law enforcement raised few suspicions; he had been nicknamed "the Teflon kid" when he was as young as fourteen. Official reports often had trouble accurately depicting the dynamic relationship among Bulger, Winter Hill, and the Italian mafia, and authorities were uncertain whether Bulger was a free agent only loosely affiliated with the Winter Hill Mob or had become more powerful than Howie Winter himself. What became increasingly apparent leading up to Winter's arrest in 1979 was that Bulger, and his close partner, Stephen Flemmi, had become the sole powers behind many of South Boston's bookmaking and loan-sharking operations, extorting heavy fines from local businesses.

In fact, the evidence used to construct the case against Howie Winter and his New Jersey counterpart, Frank Ciulla, unquestionably demonstrated Bulger's substantial involvement in the race-fixing scheme. Ciulla insisted that Bulger and Flemmi had encouraged local bookies to unwittingly bet on fixed races. When the bookies suffered heavy losses, they would become dependent on loans from Winter Hill, further extending the gang's control over the entire gambling enterprise.[17] But although Bulger and Flemmi were named as unindicted co-defendants in the 1979 case, they were never arrested or included in the final indictment. Instead, the evidence that clearly implicated Bulger as one of the main orchestrators of

62 Chapter 9

the racket would inexplicably be used to send Winter and dozens of lower-ranking lieutenants within the mob to jail for nearly a decade.

Undeterred by the failure to indict Bulger or Flemmi, the local police counterpart of the Organized Crime Task Force, headed by Lieutenant Dave Mattioli, attempted to initiate an investigation into Bulger and Flemmi, just as it had for Angiulo and Winter. The Boston police were eager to take down Bulger as his notoriety continued to grow, especially after several casual attempts to wiretap Bulger had failed. Recalling a conversation with then-Lieutenant Mattioli, Foley, perhaps with the clarity of hindsight, explained his attempts to defend the decision to investigate Bulger, saying, "[Bulger's] the biggest thing in Boston right now. Maybe ever. You know that. Everybody knows that. Just by himself, he's probably bigger than the whole LCN right now."

But the FBI resisted, and Mattioli encouraged his squad to move on and consider another level of the LCN. "They're not LCN," Mattioli explained to a disappointed Foley. "The FBI is only doing LCN."[18] At the time, that defense was not unreasonable; even in the 1980s, both local and federal attention remained largely focused on the Italian mafia, especially LCN.

The local police were not the only individuals or organizations to push for an investigation of Bulger. In 1989, Fred Wyshak joined the U.S. Attorney's Office in Boston after a decade spent prosecuting large and complex racketeering cases in Brooklyn and New Jersey. Wyshak began to ask the same question that members of Mattioli's unit had asked several years earlier: why was no one targeting Bulger?

The answer, only revealed after nearly a decade of foiled investigation attempts, would fundamentally redefine both the history of the FBI and of Boston's efforts against organized crime. For two decades, Bulger and Flemmi had been high-ranking FBI informants who provided their handlers with tips against competing mobsters as well as with lucrative—and illegal—kickbacks. In exchange, their handlers supplied information that allowed Bulger and Flemmi not only to elude capture, but also to murder other informants or competitors.

Most important, the handlers also agreed to ignore any criminal activity by the two informants in exchange for periodic information, giving Bulger and Flemmi de facto legal immunity and enabling them to commit a string of homicides. During that time period, Bulger would carry out nineteen known murders, and would consolidate a criminal empire that rivaled those of Winter Hill and the LCN combined. In short, the FBI's protection had transformed Bulger from a low-ranking gangster into one of the most powerful, violent, and well-protected mob bosses in Boston's history.

Bulger's Informant History

For the most part, only the FBI was aware of Bulger's informant status. The FBI had enlisted both Flemmi and Bulger as informants even before the creation of the joint organized crime squad: Flemmi in 1965 and Bulger in 1974. Two central questions emerge from Bulger's recruitment: why was one of the most dangerous mob criminals in Boston's history cultivated as an informant, and how did FBI safeguards fail to prevent the exchange of information for protection that characterized Bulger's relationship with his FBI handlers?

Recruiting Bulger

Bulger's recruitment was the product of two competing attitudes within the FBI toward informants. A conservative reading of the FBI's informant policy warned agents against recruiting high-ranking mobsters as informants and instructed them to avoid criminals who were likely to engage in violent crime: "Make the top guy an informant," Foley warns, "and you've given him superpowers—you've made him invulnerable to prosecution." Police treated high-ranking criminals with suspicion because they were likely to use immunity to their advantage—a status that could potentially outweigh the value of any information they might provide. On the other hand, the prestige associated with the profession of handler often fostered rivalry among FBI agents, who competed to secure high-ranking informants to curry favor with supervisors and to distinguish themselves. This attitude became the very basis of the FBI's "high-echelon" informant program.

The personality traits that had suggested to the FBI that Special Agent John Connolly might succeed in convincing Bulger to become an informant in reality became the qualities that made Connolly most vulnerable to manipulation and corruption. Several years younger than Bulger, Connolly had grown up in Southie; he would often nostalgically recall the time "Whitey" treated him and several other neighborhood boys to ice cream at a corner soda shop. In their 2012 book *Black Mass*, one of the most authoritative accounts of the Bulger affair, *Boston Globe* writers Dick Lehr and Gerard O'Neill describe Connolly as an ambitious agent who had always had a soft spot for "Whitey," and whose great admiration for Bulger divided his loyalty between the FBI and the mobster who was his boyhood hero. According to Lehr and O'Neill, several of Connolly's FBI colleagues often commented that his success with high-level informants seemed to stem from his desire to blend in with them: even before meeting Bulger, Connolly dressed and behaved more like the caricature of a criminal than a member of the FBI, wearing expensive suits, slicking his hair back, and purchasing flashy cars. Above all, Connolly was highly ambitious and eager to prove to his superiors that a fellow former resident of Southie could handle Bulger as an informant. His superiors agreed that his background gave Connolly an edge, never recognizing that Connolly's prior history with Bulger might foreshadow how the handler–informant relationship would eventually deteriorate.

The New 1980s: FBI Interference, Bulger's Immunity

When news of Bulger's informant status became public in 1995, it prompted a complete reevaluation of law enforcement's extensive investigations against the mafia and Winter Hill. Now reexamined, operations against the mob would reveal a series of small compromises manufactured by the FBI and its associates to protect Bulger from prosecution, with little to show in return.

According to Lehr and O'Neill's reconstruction of events, in his initial agreement to become an informant in 1974, Bulger stipulated unequivocally that he would not provide information about the Irish, and that his own operations were to remain undiscussed. Connolly agreed, and then presented the FBI's conditions: Bulger would provide information regarding organized crime, especially the LCN. He would avoid violent crime (agents usually expressed this rule using the familiar phrase "everything short of murder"); in return, as long as the informant relationship remained intact, Bulger could continue building his criminal enterprise uninterrupted.[19] Flemmi, who upon his own arrest would testify against Bulger, explains that Bulger decided to become an informant specifically so that he could divert attention from his own criminal empire. According to Flemmi, Bulger decided that, if necessary, he would feed useless or false information to the FBI—harmless details and mob gossip that would have little day-to-day impact on any local mob. In short, as Flemmi and other Bulger associates have revealed, Bulger entered into an agreement with the FBI to help it take down his mob competitors, particularly the Italian Mafia, in exchange for immunity and information.

64 Chapter 9

Sources dispute the extent to which Bulger felt threatened by Angiulo and the LCN in 1975. Lehr and O'Neill in particular stress that Connolly implied to Bulger that Angiulo might become an FBI informant—and thus gain the advantage of immunity—if Bulger did not act quickly.[20] Sources also disagree about exactly how helpful Bulger truly was in the dismantling of the LCN in Boston. From a logical perspective, the FBI's aggressive focus on the LCN made recruitment of Angiulo highly unlikely. More likely is that Bulger originally valued informant status for the immunity it would provide, but later recognized the opportunity to wheedle information out of the FBI about competitors and other informants. Especially telling is that, despite the FBI's warnings, Bulger would commit the first of nineteen alleged murders a mere five weeks after becoming an informant in 1974.

As the FBI's investigation into LCN progressed, Connolly continued to defend Bulger's status as an informant to his superiors even though the information Bulger provided seemed of limited value.[21] Of the hundreds of reports Connolly filed summarizing meetings with Bulger, the most significant information Bulger and Flemmi ever allegedly provided was a detailed 1981 map of the LCN's meeting spot on Prince Street, with specific suggestions about where the FBI could place electronic bugs with the least chance of detection. The advice bore fruit: the bugs formed the centerpiece of the FBI's case against LCN, and even Foley, who at the time had no idea that the FBI had relied on Bulger to place the bugs, would admire the operation for its daring. The surveillance had a profound psychological effect on the remaining members of the mafia: Angiulo had already become so paranoid about surveillance that he had disconnected his office phone and relied solely on walkie-talkies. The FBI's success in bugging the LCN's inner sanctum convinced many mob members that their dominance was, inevitably, on the decline.

The understanding that Connolly would continue to protect Bulger and Flemmi from prosecution first came into question in 1979, when the Winter Hill indictment being prepared for court included both Bulger and Flemmi's names. As subsequently revealed, law enforcement's earlier puzzlement about why Bulger was not on the indictment was well-founded. John Connolly had approached the federal prosecutor, Jeremiah O'Sullivan, the same week the indictment was due to be delivered and asked him to remove Bulger's and Flemmi's names from the indictment.[22]

Initially, as O'Sullivan would later testify, he resisted. Although he continued to place the highest priority on the case against the LCN, O'Sullivan welcomed the opportunity to remove Bulger and Flemmi from the streets, even if Bulger's involvement with Winter Hill remained unclear. But Connolly insisted that Bulger had no connection with the horse race-fixing, even though substantial evidence available to both Connolly and to O'Sullivan indicated otherwise. As Lehr and O'Neill colorfully describe, O'Sullivan continued to hesitate until Connolly revealed that Bulger was a high-value informant actively involved in the FBI's attempts to investigate the LCN. O'Sullivan promptly removed Bulger and Flemmi from the indictment. As Lehr and O'Neill explain, "O'Sullivan, the FBI could argue, should go ahead and topple the Winter Hill gang, but amid the rubble, he should just let the two lieutenants stand."[23]

In his eagerness to preserve the LCN case without jeopardizing Bulger as a source, O'Sullivan would later become part of a series of FBI compromises whose total effect provided exceptional immunity and protection for Flemmi and Bulger. Much later, when Connolly testified in his own defense, he indicated that O'Sullivan's 1979 intervention unwittingly "provided a new layer of protective veneer to the FBI's deal." As Lehr and O'Neill note, it was as if "the prosecutor had sanctified the notion that Bulger and Flemmi were protected from prosecution." Connolly himself would explain, "The first few years I met with Flemmi and Bulger, there was no understanding. The understanding didn't come until the race-fix case, and the conversations that I had with Jerry O'Sullivan."

Connolly continued actively protecting both Bulger and Flemmi from investigation and prosecution well after the 1979 indictment. This strategy of cultivating informants was explicitly authorized and encouraged by John Morris, Connolly's new supervisor and the head of the organized crime task force as of December 1977. Although in 1978 Morris criticized the high-echelon informant program on paper, and predicted that keeping Bulger as an informant might produce "legal difficulties in the near future," he continued off-the-record meetings with both Bulger and Flemmi and filed inaccurate or misplaced reports to mask the FBI's continuing reliance on Bulger and Flemmi as informants.

In 1983, state troopers finally gained authorization to bug Flemmi's car. After several foiled attempts, they orchestrated an elaborate scheme to set up Flemmi's car as stolen, tow it, and install a bug. According to a later investigation, Connolly and Morris warned Flemmi and Bulger, whom they had continued to keep apprised of the ongoing surveillance attempts.[24] When Flemmi was pulled over, he acted entirely unimpressed with the state troopers, who insisted the plates had come up as stolen and that the car had to be towed. Then, after several rounds of swearing, Flemmi sarcastically offered to drive his car up to state headquarters so the troopers could bug it. Flemmi not only identified the purpose of the stop, but also accurately identified the commanding officer leading the surveillance attempt, within seconds exposing the entire operation as a charade. The troopers were forced to abandon the effort after months of surveillance and an extensive legal battle simply to gain access to the vehicle.

In response, the FBI initiated an internal inquiry into the "stunning breach in security" that had undermined the entire state police effort, led by the new special agent in charge, Lawrence Sarhatt. Sarhatt, concerned that Connolly in particular was too close to Bulger and alarmed by the leak that had once again allowed the Irish gang to slip through law enforcement's fingers, began to suggest that Bulger and Flemmi be shut down as informants or be investigated.[25] In response, Morris and Connolly decided to link Bulger and Flemmi to the electronic surveillance of Prince Street constructing reports and memos that heavily exaggerated both informants' roles in a nearly completed effort, all of which Bulger reproduced for Sarhatt in a face-to-face meeting. When Sarhatt later approached O'Sullivan to confirm Bulger's vital role as an informant, O'Sullivan insisted that Bulger was "crucial" to the 98 Prince Street case, basing his statements on his earlier conversation with Connolly and Morris about the Winter Hill race-fixing indictment.

Bulger and Flemmi were not the only FBI informants whose FBI handlers actively protected and shielded them from prosecution. Although both Connolly and Morris went to unimaginable lengths to shield Bulger from investigation, especially by doctoring reports, memos, and documents, their behavior was not entirely unjustifiable, though certainly questionable. Connolly and Morris may well have believed they were using Bulger to fight a larger crime problem. It was not until additional facts of the case came to light that Connolly's and Morris's corruption was revealed. First, Connolly and Morris began to accept gifts and cash payments from both Bulger and Flemmi. Flemmi would later testify that Connolly accepted an estimated total of $230,000 in bribes, gifts, and other rewards, funded by an account Bulger and Flemmi had maintained specifically for bribes.[26] Suspicion grew, especially among the state and local police, when Connolly started to manifest the classic signs of corruption. He started to wear expensive suits and drive cars that seemed well outside the income of a young FBI agent. But because Connolly had secured Bulger as an informant and had his supervisor's full support he was able to avert most suspicion.

66 Chapter 9

The FBI continued its practice of foiling the state's investigations well after the state troopers' disastrous 1983 attempt to bug Flemmi. Connolly and Morris pressured agencies and squads to abandon investigations of Bulger. Oklahoma police once requested access to Bulger because of his suspected links to a series of crimes in the state; the FBI insisted that Bulger had not been involved, forcing the Oklahoma authorities to drop the case.

However, the FBI action that would mark the Bulger case as one of the most notorious in the FBI's history was the exchange of information between Connolly and Bulger that would facilitate many of Bulger's murders. Just as Connolly had warned Bulger about future surveillance and investigation, he began to warn Bulger about upcoming witnesses in investigations and to identify members of his gang who, like Bulger, had become informants.[27] Over the course of several years, Bulger murdered all three of the men Connolly had implicated: Brian Halloran, John Callahan, and Richard Castucci.

In another case, a local Boston vending machine company filed a complaint with the FBI when Bulger threatened to kill a man unless he agreed to remove his own company's vending machines from his stores and install a competitor's vending machines. This entirely legitimate complaint should have led to an indictment, except for the unvarnished accusation it leveled against Bulger, who had delivered his threat at gunpoint. Connolly, who noticed the complaint, responded by convincing the victim to drop his charges, citing the upheaval that entering witness protection would create for him and his family, hinting that Bulger would likely retaliate if the man went to court, and suggesting that any case against Bulger was likely to fail. Faced with the possible loss of his life as well as his livelihood, the man withdrew his complaint against Bulger.

Bulger carried out some of his more infamous murders—such as his strangling of Debbie Davis, one of Flemmi's girlfriends—under the assumption that the FBI would never investigate him for these disappearances and murders, if it had any reason to suspect his involvement at all. Just as often, if the FBI did ask questions, Bulger and Flemmi denied responsibility, or convincingly implicated other gangsters, leading to several false arrests and convictions.[28] In turn, Connolly relayed Bulger's defense back to the FBI, further securing Bulger's immunity from prosecution or investigation.

This exchange of information continued and formed a large portion of the criminal case later brought against Connolly, including a charge of second-degree murder that would become the subject of half a dozen civil suits from family members of the various victims. When Connolly was arrested and convicted in 2001, Donald Stern, then U.S. attorney, would soberly state during a press conference, "The handler of criminals became one himself." Morris would escape jail time, accepting immunity in exchange for his testimony.

The State's Response

During Connolly's involvement with Bulger, state troopers and the Boston police could hardly have envisioned the extent of the FBI's corruption. While it was obvious that an FBI leak was interfering with their investigations, it took several years to establish that the source was not a low-ranking FBI agent turned by the mob, but instead the handler originally tasked with collecting information from a controversial informant in exchange for protecting him.

By 1990, Fred Wyshak of the U.S. Attorney's Office in Boston continued to doggedly monitor Bulger, Flemmi, and a third associate, Frank Salemme, in an attempt to build an indictment against the three mobsters. Bulger's criminal operations involved a variety of income sources, including "bookmaking, racketeering, loansharking, drug deals, [and] extortion," but in 1993 the task force decided to focus on bookmakers. As the *Boston Globe* described the operation,

> Wyshak's strategy was to levy money laundering charges in addition to standard gambling counts against area bookies, to get them to flip and talk about organized crime figures. The stakes were raised: the bookies faced years in jail, rather than months.[29]

The strategy succeeded, building a solid and intricate RICO case against Bulger, Flemmi, and Salemme.

In 1994, as the indictments were delivered, law enforcement planned to arrest Bulger, Flemmi, and Salemme. By that point, Connolly had retired, but his relationship with Bulger and Flemmi remained largely intact. Although Connolly later insisted he never provided any advance warning, several of Bulger's associates confirm that Connolly notified Bulger and Flemmi of the pending indictments and urged them to flee just as law enforcement prepared to arrest all three men.[30]

Flemmi attempted to escape but after several days' delay was captured in Boston's popular Quincy Market. Salemme, who had never been the true focus of the indictment, escaped but was recaptured eight months later. Bulger, however, eluded capture completely. If Connolly was truly the source of the tip-off, then with one phone call Connolly had managed to unravel a years-long investigation at the seams.

The police continued to search unsuccessfully for Bulger. Meanwhile, Flemmi's capture led to the arrests of several of Bulger's associates, many of whom cooperated with the authorities after Bulger's position as an informant became public knowledge in 1995. Bulger's former girlfriend was investigated, followed by John Morris in 1997. Through the end of the 1990s, two more of Bulger's closest criminal associates, John Martorano and Kevin Weeks, were also arrested and cooperated with authorities, providing detailed accounts of Bulger's intimate relationship with the FBI.

The Consequences of the Bulger Affair, 1994–Present

Judge Mark Wolf, who oversaw the government's intricate case against Flemmi and Salemme, demanded a series of hearings that took several years to complete. A motion to suppress evidence collected while Flemmi and Bulger had still been informants served as the initial impetus for the hearings, during which several witnesses were called to testify regarding the nature of Bulger's agreement with the FBI and the promises the FBI had made to Bulger.

Judge Wolf began his 661-page ruling with the following declaration: "In 1861, Lord Acton wrote that 'everything secret degenerates, even the administration of justice.'" In the 660 pages that followed, most of the legal conclusions favored the defense, barring many pieces of evidence on which the prosecution had depended. Yet, more central to the prosecution's efforts, the factual inquiry Judge Wolf initiated would become one of the most substantive critiques of the FBI's handling of Bulger. Judge Wolf bluntly concluded that the FBI had engaged in multiple cover-ups and had passed information to Bulger that likely facilitated a series of murders.[31] He accused the FBI of promising Bulger and Flemmi immunity no matter what crimes they committed, and "describe[d] in minute detail the corruption, rule breaking, and misconduct" of the FBI. He named all eighteen agents and supervisors even peripherally involved in the Bulger affair, detailing their various degrees of involvement. He methodically proved that O'Sullivan had known about Bulger's informant status since 1979 (despite several public statements to the contrary), and identified Connolly as the most likely source of the tip that had permitted Bulger to avoid investigation in the late 1980s.

68 Chapter 9

In the immediate aftermath of Wolf's 1999 ruling, John Connolly was arrested and indicted for rack-eteering and second-degree murder.[32] Between the state and federal charges, he was sentenced to fifty years in prison—a sentence that, at age 72, he is still completing. Following his conviction, the families of Bulger's victims, as well as the families of those wrongfully convicted of Bulger's crimes, aggressively sued the federal government over the FBI's role in Bulger's activities, earning over $120 million in civil damages.

2011 Capture and Trial

The story of Whitey Bulger might have ended there. But on June 22, 2011, Bulger and his long-time girlfriend, Catherine Greig, were arrested in Santa Monica, California, after evading law enforcement for seventeen years. Transporting Bulger to Boston's waterfront federal courthouse required the authorities to shut down part of the Boston Harbor. Bulger was indicted under RICO on a series of racketeering charges involving narcotics, money laundering, and extortion. He was also charged with nineteen counts of murder. Fred Wyshak would return as part of a three-man team of prosecutors that set out to prove a case whose original indictment had been issued over two decades earlier.

The trial began on June 12, 2013. The prosecution's case in chief described Bulger's criminal net-work as well as his involvement in nineteen murders and a series of rackets and extortion charges, "his former partners in crime parading to the witness stand to testify against him."[33] Flemmi, Martorano, Kevin Weeks, and a number of other associates would repeat many of the blistering accusations that had originated in the Wolf hearings: they admitted that they had all been members of Bulger's extensive organized crime network, that they had witnessed or learned of many of the murders Bulger was accused of committing or having others commit, and that Bulger had been an informant. Other witnesses spoke candidly about the payments Bulger had demanded in exchange for the right to do business in Bulger's territory, calling Bulger's criminal network "an umbrella of extortion." Bulger remained largely silent during this testimony, disrupting court only a handful of times to angrily exchange expletives with Kevin Weeks and Stephen Flemmi after their testimony.

Although many anticipated that Bulger would testify in his own defense, he elected at the end of the trial not to testify. As a result, Bulger's defense focused exclusively on calling attention to the circum-stantial nature of the evidence corroborating many of the oldest murders, while insisting that Bulger had never actually been an informant. In his exchange with the presiding judge after announcing his decision, he insisted that he had "been choked off from having an opportunity to give an adequate defense." Bulger maintained that the now-deceased prosecutor involved in the Winter Hill indictment, Jeremiah O'Sullivan, had given him immunity in exchange for an agreement to protect the prosecutor. No mention was made of Bulger's well-documented status as an informant, which his counsel vigorously contested throughout the trial. Bulger concluded, "As far as I'm concerned, I didn't get a fair trial, and this is a sham. And do what yous want with me." A prior ruling from the presiding judge had prevented the defense from arguing that Bulger had been given a "license to kill."

The jury began its deliberations in early August and concluded five days later. Bulger was found guilty of thirty-one counts of his indictment and convicted of eleven of nineteen murders. The jury stated that there was insufficient evidence for seven of the remaining eight murder charges, and made no finding in the final murder—that of Debbie Davis. On November 14, 2013, Bulger was sentenced to two consecu-tive life sentences plus an additional five years, and ordered to forfeit $25.2 million to the government and pay $19.5 million to the victims and their families.[34] While the sentence assuredly means Bulger will die in prison, the civil penalties were "largely symbolic ... law enforcement has not uncovered anywhere near that amount of money stashed away by Bulger." During Bulger's sentencing, U.S. District Court Judge Denise Casper noted, "The testimony of human suffering that you and your associates inflicted on others was at times agonizing to hear and painful to watch ... The scope, the callousness, the depravity of your crimes, are almost unfathomable."

Conclusion

The Wolf ruling, the aftermath of the 1994 investigation, and the publicity surrounding Bulger's conviction generated scathing analysis of the FBI's original guidelines for handlers tasked with high-echelon informants, the corruption that enabled Bulger to act with impunity, and the insular qualities that encouraged the FBI to defend Bulger even as evidence of his wrongdoing piled higher. In many ways, the Bulger case also became a sobering reminder of the shortcomings of Robert Kennedy's campaign against organized crime, initiated three decades before. The specialized structures and federal task forces designed to investigate criminals such as Bulger had actively assisted him, shielded him, and abetted his escape. Enthusiasm for taking down one group of criminals transformed the FBI into the source of immunity for a man who would remain on the FBI's Most Wanted list for over a decade.

Notes

* To avoid any apparent use of non-public information about the Bulger case, Stephen Heymann did not participate in its research and writing.

1 Foley and Sedgwick, *Most Wanted* (New York: Touchstone Publishing, a Division of Simon & Schuster, 2016), 13.
2 Foley and Sedgwick, *Most Wanted*, 17.
3 Jay S. Albanese, "North American Organised Crime," *Global Crime*, Vol. 6, No. 1 (2004): 8–18.
4 Peter Mass, *The Valachi Papers* (New York: HarperCollins, 2003), 37.
5 Ibid.
6 Special Senate Comm. to Investigate Organized Crime in Interstate Commerce, *The Kefauver Committee Report on Organized Crime in Interstate Commerce* 106–13 (1951) ("People everywhere are pleading for a means of keeping alert to crime conditions and avoiding a return to the state of public complacency and indifference under which gangsterism has thrived for so long. The demand for a permanent force that can, in some measure, replace this committee must be met.").
7 Robert F. Kennedy, "Statement by Attorney General Robert F. Kennedy to the Permanent Subcommittee on Investigations of the Senate Government Operations Committee" (speech, Washington, DC, September 25, 1963), Department of Justice, www.justice.gov/ag/rfkspeeches/1963/09-25-1963.pdf. http://perma.cc/YA9A-89SL.
8 Dick Lehr and Gerard O'Neill, *Black Mass: Whitey Bulger, the FBI, and a Devil's Deal* (New York: PublicAffairs Store, 2012), 659–660.
9 *Whitey Bulger: The Making of a Monster.* Documentary Film. Boston, MA: Northern Light Productions.
10 T.J. English, "Irish vs. Irish," in *Paddy Whacked: The Untold Story of the Irish American Gangster* (New York: HarperCollins, 2005), 100.
11 Ibid.; Foley and Sedgwick, *Most Wanted*, 24–26.
12 Ibid.
13 Foley and Sedgwick, *Most Wanted*, 30.
14 Ibid., 1217–1218.

70 Chapter 9

15 Lehr and O'Neill, *Black Mass: Whitey Bulger*, 1189–1191.

16 Foley and Sedgwick, *Most Wanted*, 28.

17 Ibid.

18 Ibid.

19 Lehr and O'Neill, *Black Mass: Whitey Bulger*, 1750–1752. (Whereas Flemmi would continue to insist that the FBI had assured them that they would "look the other way on everything short of murder," Morris would later state that he had no memory of making any such statement or assurance.)

20 Ibid., 264–267.

21 *United States v. Francis P. Salemme, James J. Bulger, Stephen Flemmi et al.*, 94-10287 U.S. Ma. (1998) (Wolf, Memorandum of Order) [hereinafter "Wolf Report"].

22 Ibid.

23 Ibid., 1197–1198.

24 Ibid.

25 Ibid., 1689–1690.

26 Ibid.

27 Lehr and O'Neill, *Black Mass: Whitey Bulger*, 5282–5284.

28 Ibid.

29 Milton J. Valencia, "Bulger Trial is Culmination of Lengthy, Dogged Pursuit," *Boston Globe*, June 2, 2013, accessed July 2013, www.bostonglobe.com/metro/2013/06/01/prosecutors-james-whitey-bulger-were-there-onset-investigation/YYyGh3BsFe5ZHdwwKYYlGO/story.html. http://perma.cc/A6DX-37JT.

30 Lehr and O'Neill, *Black Mass: Whitey Bulger*, 100; "Wolf Report."

31 Ibid.

32 Foley and Sedgwick, *Most Wanted*, 286–287.

33 Katharine Q. Seelye, "Bulger Declines to Testify, But Gets Something Off His Mind: 'This Is a Sham,'" *New York Times*, August 8, 2013. www.nytimes.com/2013/08/03/us/james-whitey-bulger-trial.html. http://perma.cc/BE79-W2GN.

34 Ibid.

PART THREE
Globalization

Introduction

We have seen in Chapter 7 that one of the plausible explanations for the success of U.S. law enforcement in the late 20th century was that the world was changing rapidly in ways that undermined the businesses of La Cosa Nostra in the United States. The governments' lotteries were taking over from "numbers" gambling; drugs from Latin America were replacing Sicilian heroin; labor unions were losing their powers; and loan-sharking was faced with the competition of a multitude of credit cards. Three decades later the world had, of course, continued to change in ways that affected the businesses of organized crime, but this time sometimes to their advantage.

One major advantage for organized crime, the effect of becoming transnational, is explored in Chapter 10. A crime planned and partly executed from a "home" or "haven" state ("H") for the organized crime group might ultimately cause harm and losses in other "victim" ("V") states. Efforts to identify the perpetrators would naturally center in "V," where the crime took place and did its damage. Little investigative energy would be spent in H: (a) by H's police, for H was not harmed; or (b) by V's police whom international law forbid to investigate beyond V's borders.

Chapter 11 shows that treaties of extradition or mutual legal assistance might create legal obligations for H to assist. But there are many reasons why H might not want to help, many technical exceptions to the promise to help, and, in any event, any obligations of H depend on V first identifying H as the perpetrator's home without having a right to investigate in H. All these problems for V are advantages for the organized crime group.

But the advantages transnational crime enjoys when it works across borders depend on the states divided by borders remaining distrustful of each other, indifferent to the other's welfare, and jealous of credit flowing to another law enforcement force. As Chapters 12 and 13 explain, and document with a case study involving the United States and Colombia, the advantages to organized crime of globalization tend to shrink and then disappear when two law enforcement teams from two or more countries have trust, concern for the other, and unconcern about locating credit.

10
GOING INTERNATIONAL

Introduction

We have seen in the previous chapters that the United States has been successful in dealing with organized crime because of new investigative techniques, new statutes like RICO and money laundering, an organizational structure that permits sustained focus and growing intelligence about organized crime groups, and an effective, honest, and unintimidated law enforcement and court system. Even then, we also saw in Chapter 6 that the United States was blessed by favorable conditions for dealing with an organized crime group like the LCN: new, lawful competition for the businesses such as gambling and lending which the group had hoped to monopolize; new illegal competition in the sale of a drug; a weakening of its capacity for labor extortion; and a loss of community support. All of these actions and conditions interfered with the primary businesses of organized crime: monopolizing a lucrative market in contraband or engaging in extortion.

Many countries do not have the capacities or conditions that we have described. Without those capacities these countries are likely to become "haven" states where native organized crime groups can grow and thrive and where foreign organized crime groups may move because of their comparative safety from the dangers of law enforcement.

For organized crime groups, the only drawback in locating in these host states is that the most lucrative markets in contraband are likely to exist in wealthier countries with far more effective law enforcement (the "victim" states). When an organized crime group like the Sinaloa Cartel makes arrangements to buy the contraband from organizations in one area and then makes arrangements with other organizations to distribute it in the wealthier "victim" market, it creates a global business broadly similar to the business of a globalized seller of legal goods.

What can the victim state, in this case a wealthy, contraband-purchasing country such as the United States, do in these circumstances? There are four major alternatives a victim state has for dealing with transnational organized crime organizations.

First, it could seek to investigate and prosecute by itself any of the activities of the group that are sufficiently tied to its sovereignty to be subject to its laws.

74 Chapter 10

Second, it could use its diplomatic and economic powers to press a reluctant haven state either to investigate and prosecute groups targeting the victim state or to use military force against them. It might even go further and pressure the haven state to take extra-legal steps, declaring domestic "war" on the organized crime group, perhaps even using vigilantes or rival groups to assist its military, as we saw with the joint Colombian/U.S. initiative against Escobar in Colombia.

Third, if the haven state is incapable of providing meaningful assistance, the victim state could help develop adequate law enforcement institutions or military capacities in the haven state. Examples would be the relatively massive training of law enforcement and equipping of national security forces in Colombia ("Project Colombia") and in Mexico (the "Merida Plan").

A fourth and final option is to try to reduce the profit from sales of contraband in the victim state. The profit earned by the organized crime group depends on monopolizing or restricting competitive sales of an illicit contraband product. There would be far less incentive to bear the risks and costs of smuggling in a more competitive market where the profits were far less. For example, if the United States continues to legalize the production and distribution of marijuana, it would cease to be a profitable illegal Mexican export. Similarly, if we were to permit freer transportation of cocaine from Colombia across the Caribbean, the business of smuggling it in from Mexico would dry up. But either plan would increase the availability and reduce the cost of these drugs in the United States. Of course, if the United States were to reduce the size of its demand, that too would reduce the profits to foreign suppliers from sales. But as we have discussed in previous chapters, various initiatives to reduce drug use have proven relatively ineffective thus far.

Finally, we should note that the attractiveness of the first three options depends upon the haven state's willingness to cooperate. That cooperation cannot be taken for granted when the haven state benefits from a substantial flow of money from the illicit sales. Even then, its fear of losing control of the country or of becoming itself the victim of spreading sales of dangerous contraband may cause it to cooperate.

The Constraints of International Law: A Hypothetical Example

Let us turn to the first option. Can the United States, as the victim state, punish or deter organized crime activities from a haven state in the most straightforward way—by seeking to investigate and prosecute the activity itself? This question immediately raises matters of legality under both international law and the U.S. Constitution. Consider the following hypothetical example:

> Jorge, a Mexican-American, is the leader of a faction of the Gulf organized crime group which transports cocaine into the United States for sale. The United States has discovered that, hoping to broaden his inventory, Jorge will travel to Iran by way of Rome to make arrangements for the purchase of heroin as part of a plan to open a new line of drugs: Gulf heroin to be sold in the United States. The U.S. Drug Enforcement Agency has proposed investigating the business associates he meets with in Rome, where he plans to stay for the better part of a week. Ordinary physical surveillance in public places and casual interviews will be used. But the DEA also plans to search Jorge's apartment and to monitor his telephone calls while he is in Rome.
>
> At the end of the week, DEA agents plan to apprehend Jorge, interrogate him without Miranda warnings, and put him, handcuffed and guarded, on a commercial flight from Rome to New York where they plan to charge him with conspiracy to traffic in illegal drugs. Alternatively, the DEA could ask the Italians to arrest and then extradite Jorge to the United States.

Assume that, as legal advisers to the DEA, we have been asked to give our views on any problems of illegality that may be involved in DEA's plan. It will be clarifying to divide the problems into two parts: international law restrictions and U.S. constitutional law requirements.

Constraints of International Law

Let us start with restrictions imposed by international law, which comes in two major forms: customary international law that has been accepted by enough states and other authorities to be binding on all; and treaty obligations, legally binding promises between two or more countries made either on a bilateral or multilateral basis.

Domestic criminal law in most countries requires a statute prohibiting certain conduct and only then an investigation into whether the statute was violated, followed by an arrest if it was, and then a trial. But a U.S. statute may not alone create law that other states will recognize. Customary international law forbids the United States trying to prohibit certain conduct taking place in, for example, Italy, except under specified circumstances; or the United States sending its police to investigate and arrest in another state, without the latter's permission. Customary international law forbids a victim state to intrude in these ways on another state's sovereignty. In particular, it separately restricts (1) the right of one nation to enact "extraterritorial" statutes prohibiting certain activities taking place wholly in other states; and (2) it forbids one state to investigate or arrest in another state to enforce its statutes.

The latter restrictions are the more severe. Under customary international law, U.S. agents cannot even politely interview willing witnesses in another country without the consent of that state's government. U.S. agents certainly can't execute a search or an arrest in Rome, as DEA plans in our hypothetical. On the other hand, the United States can charge Jorge with an extraterritorial U.S. crime in these circumstances because Jorge's actions are intended to have effects in the United States. After all, in this case, Jorge is plotting in Rome to sell drugs in the United States, a U.S. crime of conspiracy, a culminating part of which was intended to occur in the United States even though the early stages took place abroad.

An extraterritorial prohibition of certain conduct (such as plotting outside of the victim country to sell illegal drugs in the victim country) is consistent with customary international law if it satisfies any one of four traditional grounds for establishing the right to regulate activities in a foreign country: (1) If the activities are intended to have an effect within the victim country, they will be considered the same as actions taking place within the victim state and such territorial claims legitimate the right of the victim state to prohibit or regulate the conduct. (Jorge's plans satisfy this category.) (2) If the suspect is a citizen of the victim state, he can be required to obey its laws even when he is in another state, although the United States rarely asserts this power. (Jorge is a U.S. person.) (3) If the suspect's actions are intended to endanger significant functions of the victim state (i.e., if they rise to a national security threat), the "protective" principle will allow the victim state to forbid such activities even by foreigners outside its borders (not applicable to Jorge). Finally, (4) if the activities are recognized by almost all states as posing unusual threats to the legal arrangements that have acquired particular importance to international relations and structures, any state in the world may be able to prosecute under the principle of "universality." (Torture or piracy would fit into this category if a plan to commit a "universal" crime were established.)

76 Chapter 10

The right to make Jorge's conduct criminal under the first category has important consequences even though DEA may not investigate or arrest in a foreign state. As a start, the DEA might not need to investigate Jorge in Rome if it already has enough evidence found within the United States to prosecute him. As to arrest and trial, the United States could also use violation of the extraterritorial statute to extradite Jorge for trial in the United States (a subject described in the next chapter). Alternatively, Jorge might travel to a state from which the United States could extradite him or, with the consent of that state, seize him. Even seizing Jorge secretly and illegally in Italy does not interfere with our right to try him in U.S. courts under familiar doctrines of customary international law, although it would have severe diplomatic repercussions.

Legality Under U.S. Law

Even where international law allows law enforcement by the agents of the "victim" state, such as the United States in our example, further questions arise about whether American standards of civil liberties, found in the 4th and 5th amendments to the U.S. Constitution, apply to searches and interrogations of either aliens or U.S. persons abroad.

Although the 2008 Foreign Intelligence Surveillance Act Amendments authorized and mandated a FISA warrant for intelligence investigations in these circumstances, the result for criminal investigations is still unclear. The Federal Court of Appeals for the Second Circuit partially addressed the latter issue in the *El-Hage* case, saying that any such search must satisfy the 4th Amendment requirement of "reasonableness" but not its Warrant clause. Were Jorge a Mexican, he would have no 4th Amendment rights while outside the United States (*U.S. v. Verdugo*).

One further question remains concerning partnerships between countries to investigate international organized crime. There is little guidance in either the statutes or constitutional decisions as to what level of involvement by the U.S. officials would make the search or electronic surveillance by officials in Italy—the Italian police in our example—the responsibility of the U.S. for purposes of the 4th or 5th amendments. If, for example, the DEA asked the Italian police to search or wiretap Jorge for us, the resulting search would clearly be considered a DEA action. If, however, the DEA simply told the Italian police of DEA's interest in Jorge, and trusted that the tradition of reciprocal assistance it had cultivated with its counterparts in Italy would bear fruit, that might not constitute DEA action.

As to an interrogation after taking a U.S. person such as Jorge into custody, the 5th amendment requirements of *Miranda* would continue to apply. Under customary international law Jorge could not be detained or interrogated in Italy without the permission of the Italian government. Even with that permission, under the U.S. Constitution he would have to be advised of his *Miranda* rights to counsel and to remain silent. The same might be true even of a non-U.S. person interrogated in Italy prior to a trial in the United States.

In short, international law and the rules for application abroad of U.S. constitutional and statutory law will greatly complicate the task of addressing transnational organized crimes without treaties of law enforcement cooperation. Such treaties, as we shall now see, can help but do not eliminate this difficulty.

11

INTERNATIONAL LAW ENFORCEMENT COOPERATION PURSUANT TO TREATIES

A state that is the "victim" of transnational shipment of illegal drugs wants to use its criminal laws to incapacitate, deter, or prevent organized criminal groups, operating from a "haven" state, from shipping drugs or other contraband into its territory. That requires either the (usually less motivated) haven state being willing and able to arrest the suspects and bring them and evidence against them into its courts or the (usually more motivated) victim state being able to obtain from the haven state the cooperation necessary to bring the suspects and the evidence into the victim state's territory and court system.

We have seen that customary international law forbids a victim state from, on its own, arresting an individual abroad and bringing him within its borders for trial; and it forbids any form of investigation by a victim state in a foreign country (such as the haven state) without the consent of that government, which is rarely given. International criminal law enforcement thus comes to depend largely on the police, prosecutors, and courts of the haven state being motivated and willing to discover, seize, and deliver the evidence and the suspect to the victim state. The haven state's motivation, captured in advance in extradition treaties and mutual legal assistance treaties, is to receive reciprocal cooperation on a future occasion and to build diplomatic bonds.

An extradition treaty is an agreement that, in specified circumstances and on request, one state (the "requested" state) will arrest and send to another (the "requesting" state) an individual who has committed a crime against the laws of the requesting state. The United States will not arrest and extradite an individual within our borders without such a treaty. Nor will we sign such treaties with countries to which we are unwilling to send individuals, perhaps because we reject their political and legal structures.

Even when there is a treaty between two states a problem remains. Extradition treaties leave to the requested haven state a great deal of formal leeway and much informal discretion. The treaties almost always require that the conduct be a crime in both the victim and the haven state (the "requesting" and the "requested" state). For some of the most powerful U.S. statutes against organized crime, such as RICO, this may in itself pose problems for extradition, since many states do not have comparable crimes. In addition, many states will not extradite their nationals, regarding the right not to be sent to another state for trial as one of the fundamental rights of their citizens. All extradition treaties exclude extradition

78 Chapter 11

for "political" crimes. Although provisions in some extradition treaties can be more specific, there is often no significant agreement on the meaning of this term "political." The requesting state must intend to prosecute under a statute that the haven state agrees is within the requesting state's international jurisdiction to proscribe conduct, a subject we examined in the last chapter. The requested state can choose to prosecute in its own courts rather than extradite if it has jurisdiction over the crime the requesting state wants to try. It can also avoid extradition if it instead charges and tries the suspect, in its own courts, for a different pending crime. Finally, extradition must be approved not only by judicial officials certifying to its compliance with the treaty but also by the foreign ministry, which will assess diplomatic considerations, generally after the courts have already ruled on legality.

With all these caveats, there is frequently room to avoid extradition. Members of organized crime groups generally prefer to be tried in their home states, if corruption and intimidation, or a more generous pattern of punishment promise a more favorable outcome. Thus criminals may threaten the haven state or its citizens with violence in order to get that state to avoid extradition. This was the case in Colombia with Pablo Escobar, in Germany with the Hamadei case, and in France with the trial of Georges Ibrahim Abdollah. In all three, threats had some successes. Even if all the conditions are met, threats are ignored, and individuals are extradited, they can only be tried in the victim state for crimes for which they were extradited. The rules of "specialty" forbid trying them for any other crime. Many of these obstacles to extradition can be exploited by a reluctant haven state to deny a request for extradition.

For the victim state requesting extradition, meeting these many conditions will often take a substantial amount of time and effort. In the meantime, an extradition treaty permits the requesting state to ask for the provisional arrest, by the requested state, of the suspect. That gives the requesting state more time to file a formal document specifying the crimes and the facts on which it is relying. Recent treaties allow the formal request to move directly between justice ministries rather than first to a foreign ministry which sends it to another state's foreign ministry to be relayed to the latter's justice ministry or courts. In the European Union, the process has been expedited by authorizing a European arrest warrant. A judge in one European Union state can simply issue such a warrant if the crime is serious enough, and the warrant will be executed by police in another European state who will then deliver the individual arrested to the issuing court.

The United States has a large set of extradition treaties with a number of nations. Despite their weaknesses, these treaties can assist in getting a person suspected of violating U.S. law into the United States from a haven abroad and before a U.S. court. But what about the evidence outside the U.S. borders? As we saw in Chapter 9, international law does not allow U.S. agents to gather evidence in foreign countries—evidence that is often needed to ensure a successful prosecution.

Ideally, to minimize the effect of the advantages that national borders provide to criminals, the U.S. and its close allies would have a form of search warrant analogous to the European arrest warrant for gathering evidence on foreign soil. For example, a bilateral agreement could allow, with a judge's approval, police of the haven state to gather certain evidence needed for the trial in the victim state or, still more useful, authorize investigators from the victim state to gather evidence in the haven state.

While such an agreement would be helpful in combating international organized crime, no such agreement now exists. We saw in Chapter 10 that U.S. investigations in a foreign country cannot take place without the agreement of that country; customary international law forbids any investigation outside a state's own borders without the consent of the state where the investigation is to take place. Moreover, states are jealous of their police powers and unlikely to agree to an independent investigation within their boundaries by the law enforcement of any other state. Even the efforts of the members of the European community to cooperate on law enforcement through the creation of Europol resulted primarily in a mechanism for communal information exchange. Europol can propose the creation of joint investigative teams for a specific case, but that is rarely done.

What remains are Mutual Legal Assistance Treaties (MLATs); agreements that the country where the evidence is located will use its own investigative capabilities to assist another state, at the latter's request, in gathering the information that the other state needs to solve a crime, justify an arrest, extradite for trial, or permit a conviction with adequate, usable evidence. MLATs are slow in operation, although far better than their predecessors: "letters rogatory." MLATs allow direct communication with the law enforcement authorities of another state; letters rogatory required all such cooperation to be arranged through foreign ministries and executed by courts. Still, MLATs inhibit the flexibility and shifting of direction that investigators need when working "on the ground," because everything must be done in writing and each change delays the pending investigation or prosecution. While far from perfect, MLATs are the major formal device available to investigators of international crime.

Given the cumbersome and largely ineffective formal system of international law enforcement cooperation, it is therefore not surprising that U.S. investigative agencies acquire much of their information informally through friendship and reciprocity among police agencies of different countries. (This process working at its best is illustrated in the final case study, an account of the joint U.S. and Colombian pursuit of drug traffickers.) The United States has FBI and DEA representatives (called attachés) in a sizable number of countries. The attachés receive requests from the host country for investigative information within the United States and relay requests from the United States to foreign police departments for investigative help. The state requested to deliver this investigative assistance may, or may not, need a separate basis—more than a desire to cooperate—under its own applicable law for taking the steps requested.

Both bilateral treaties and informal attaché relationships have the advantages that come with being able to choose with whom we want to work closely in an area as sensitive as law enforcement. They have the disadvantage of including only those particular states with which we have signed a treaty or developed close police arrangements for mutual cooperation.

Multinational treaties (conventions) help to fill the remaining gaps. Modern multi-state conventions against particular forms of conduct frequently include provisions for mutual legal assistance at the investigative stage as well as provisions for extradition. For example, the Convention Against Organized Crime requires each member state to criminalize organized crime, money laundering, corruption and obstruction of justice and also to extradite and provide mutual legal assistance for these crimes. It also includes provisions for forfeiting the proceeds of organized crime at another signatory state's request.

Even with these treaties and arrangements, victim states are frequently stymied in international investigations. Why does this set of arrangements not enable a victim state (for example, the state to which contraband is sent from a haven state) to prosecute organized crime as effectively as we saw U.S. officials doing domestically in Part Two? The answers are found both in the capacities and the motivation of the haven state.

Take capacity first. In locating its activities, organized crime groups look for states with weak or corrupt law enforcement. Mexico, for example, is estimated to solve less than two percent of its crimes. Among the reasons for this have been under-trained, under-paid, under-equipped, and under-empowered municipal police, who are distrusted by an uncooperating populace. Mexico's investigative and trial procedures are changing but are still largely archaic; its prosecutors and judges, often unprofessional. These problems put Mexican law enforcement at a particular disadvantage when the crimes are committed by a dangerous, wealthy, and sophisticated organization.

80 Chapter 11

Now turn to motivation. As we saw in earlier chapters, a large portion of the proceeds of Mexico's drug cartels is spent on corruption designed to deter law enforcement and its administrative and political leaders from pursuing the cartels. Furthermore, the overriding motivation of almost any law enforcement system is to solve and punish crimes occurring in its own country, not those occurring in a foreign nation.

Moreover, it takes more motivation to pursue a costly and difficult case of organized crime than a simpler, less time-consuming case. Motivation of law enforcement everywhere is weakened by the difficulty of making a case: both factual complexity and intimidation of witnesses makes a successful prosecution for organized crime far less likely. Motivation falls precipitously when police, prosecutors, and judges are intimidated or believe that their colleagues are corrupt.

For all these reasons, a haven state is likely to take advantage of the many gaps in the fabric of cooperation spun out of treaty obligations to extradite or assist a victim state. Thus, the system is likely to fail unless both states are threatened similarly by the same organization, both have the capacities needed to respond, and both share the same motivation to work together to meet the common danger—an unusual situation we will now describe and analyze.

12

THE COLOMBIAN CONNECTION

A Truly Cooperative Solution for an International Problem

Some of the advantages which organized crime groups gain when they begin to operate outside their country's borders can be mitigated by highly informal cooperation between law enforcement forces in the haven and victim states. Indeed, when law enforcement teams in multiple countries enjoy a high measure of mutual trust, feel concern for each other's welfare, and have a decently limited interest in which state and which organization receives personal credit, these teams can draw on the most flexible, effective, and unimpeachable part of each system to successfully stop transnational organized crime groups that no single state could handle alone.

The description of Operation Beanpot which follows is an example of exactly how this works when it works. In it we shall see the law enforcement teams training together; learning and utilizing their knowledge of which state's law is most permissive for gathering particular evidence; selecting the state of trial in light of the risks of corruption and intimidation and the difficulties of the procedural complexities which each system has created, and much more. In short, so long as their goal is held very much in common, Colombia can learn to utilize the advantages of American teams in investigation and trial, and Americans can learn to use the advantages of Colombian teams. Both can escape the most serious disadvantages of working alone on the case; each can overcome the disadvantages of both cumbersome treaty arrangements, untrusted law enforcement participants in their country, and difficulties posed by domestic law. It is to point out these possibilities that we turn to the story of Operation Beanpot.

While most international narcotics investigations start with drug seizures, Operation Beanpot—one of the most successful international narco-trafficking investigations in the last decade[1]—started with money. Following the money proved fruitful for the DEA, but it was the unprecedented level of cooperation between the DEA and law enforcement in Colombia and other countries that led to the capture, extradition, and prosecution of major Colombian drug traffickers in this case.

The operation began in early 2005 with a Venezuelan "Peso Broker"—a money launderer who was part of an extensive underworld financial network that funneled drug proceeds from the United States to Colombia. Known as the "Black Market Peso Exchange,"[2] this network used drug money (U.S. dollars) to purchase goods (such as electronics or liquor) in the United States; the goods were

82 Chapter 12

then shipped to Colombia where they were sold for pesos (either by middlemen or by the drug cartels themselves).

When the Peso Broker, known as "Confidential Informant #1" (CI-1), agreed to work with the DEA's Boston office in exchange for a monetary reward, Special Agent Dennis Barton realized the agency had something big. As a key player in international money laundering, CI-1 had contacts at every level of the trafficking world: Colombian producers, Mexican smugglers, and American distributors. Given CI-1's connections, Barton and his colleague, Special Agent John Grella, hoped that following the money trail would lead the DEA to major narco-traffickers.

Barton and Grella believed the best way to arrest the top people in the drug trade was for DEA agents to become part of the operation, in this case posing as money launderers. Such a proposal understandably required approval from high-ranking officials at the Justice Department. The DEA designated Operation Beanpot as an undercover "Attorney General Exempt Operation" (AGEO), which would allow the agents to break certain laws for a limited period of time in order to solve a larger crime.[3] In this case, the DEA team would be allowed to launder money for the drug cartels and take a commission for its work. DEA would use the money to fund the entire investigation. Selectively, DEA would "seize" transfers, thus taking more money away from the traffickers (by the end of the investigation, Operation Beanpot had confiscated approximately $10 million in drug proceeds from the cartels).[4] But for several years the operation would allow most proceeds to flow from the United States to Colombia so that DEA could learn the structure of the trafficking organization.

Attorney General Alberto Gonzalez approved the AGEO request. Working with Assistant U.S. Attorney Zachary Hafer, the Boston DEA office launched the operation. Using CI-1 to make introductions by phone to narco-traffickers in the Boston area, the case's main undercover government agent (UC-1) began picking up drug proceeds in 2005 and laundering the funds before sending them to Colombia using special DEA bank accounts. The quantities involved were small at first: $5,000 or $10,000 per pick-up. Slowly, however, UC-1 gained the trust of the other drug traffickers, and the size of the money pick-ups increased. Eventually, UC-1 handled payments as large as $200,000 per transaction.

After two years of laundering money from the Boston area and wiring it directly to Colombian bank accounts, Operation Beanpot achieved its first big break. In March 2007, UC-1's contacts asked him to travel to the Bahamas to launder money from local traffickers. Once there, UC-1 was given several Colombian cell phone numbers to use to coordinate payments. This was the first direct connection to individuals in Colombia that the investigation had yielded; thus far agents had discovered only anonymous shell corporations and bank accounts. Although the DEA agents were not fully certain at the time, they suspected that the large size of the money pick-up (over $200,000) signaled that the cell phones belonged to the major Colombian narco-traffickers who actually "owned" the drugs.[5] With the cell phone numbers in hand, Hafer and the DEA agents knew that it was time to bring international partners into the investigation and to ask for assistance from Colombia; specifically, they needed help monitoring the conversations taking place on the suspects' cell phones.

The DEA and Colombian Law Enforcement

The DEA had long enjoyed an excellent working relationship with Colombian law enforcement. For example, Colombia was one of only a handful of countries that allowed U.S. counterparts to carry firearms on its soil. In addition, the DEA had field offices in both Bogotá and Cartagena, with over three hundred agents permanently assigned to Colombia and hundreds more who rotated in and out of the country each year.[6]

As noted, law enforcement agents may only exercise police functions in another nation if that country consents. While the DEA agents in Colombia had substantial latitude, they did not work alone (nor would they want to do so and sacrifice the benefits of cooperation). Instead, the DEA built a working relationship with specially vetted Colombian law enforcement personnel from two agencies: the Colombian National Police (CNP) and the Administrative Department of Security (DAS). DEA's ongoing work with the CNP and DAS allowed U.S. investigators to pursue cases in Colombia without, as Hafer said, "pushing our luck and making [Colombian law enforcement] think they're just doing our bidding. It's a real partnership."

However, DEA chose few Colombian law enforcement personnel for these teams, because of concerns about corruption. Fears of government collaboration with violent organized crime groups had pervaded operations in the early 1990s, when the United States and Colombia worked together with the infamous and violent Cali Cartel to hunt down the notorious drug kingpin Pablo Escobar. Although Colombia had made much progress since then, corruption remained a major problem in all levels of the government, including the police, prosecutors, and the judiciary.[7]

In the world of undercover (or "sting") operations, where government agents operating under cover of a false identity deal closely with hardened criminals, deciding whom to trust is vital; choosing incorrectly could endanger not only the investigation, but also the lives of the undercover agents. In this case, DEA agents relied on their Colombian counterparts to help determine when informants were telling the truth and which ones could be trusted. While Colombia had not yet succeeded in conducting a wholesale cleanup of its law enforcement organizations, the government had created specially vetted teams to work with U.S. agents in the country. Officers from the CNP and DAS underwent extensive background checks before selection, and ongoing integrity monitoring afterwards, including polygraph examinations every week. The CNP and DAS officers chosen enjoyed a collegial working relationship with their American counterparts. As Hafer explained: "They work long hours together, they know each other by their first names, they grab a beer after work together." Indeed, the recollections of the agents in this case indicate that drinks after work in Bogotá's upscale Zona Rosa neighborhood appear to have done as much to facilitate international cooperation as any formal training program run by the U.S. Department of Justice.

The Wiretaps

Hafer, Barton, and Grella wanted to monitor conversations on the cell phone numbers given to UC–1 in the Bahamas, but the DEA had no authority to conduct wiretapping operations in Colombia—they would have to take place under the auspices of Colombian law enforcement. Even though the investigation would be conducted only by the vetted Colombian teams, trust remained an issue; Operation Beanpot would be ruined if corrupt Colombian police officials tipped off the owners of the cell phones. Two years of work would be lost, turning Operation Beanpot into a failed AGEO that helped traffickers more than law enforcement. Hafer knew the risks:

> Were we concerned about trust issues? Sure, of course, at first. Anyone during an international investigation would be. But on this one, I had to defer to the judgment of the DEA agents on the

case. They were the ones who worked with these guys in Colombia. And if they were willing to trust them, that was good enough for me.

After discussing the issue with the DEA squad, Hafer agreed that the cell phone numbers should be given to vetted DAS and CNP officials. The opportunity to "catch the big fish" outweighed the risks that might arise from sharing information.

In 2007, Colombian law enforcement started wiretaps on the cell phone numbers provided by UC-1. Unlike in the United States, wiretap orders were easy to obtain under Colombian law, and only required prior approval by a prosecutor, or *fiscal*, not by a judge. The investigation eventually had lawful wiretap orders for more than 200 Colombian cell phones. Not only did the vetted Colombian officers prove trustworthy with the narco-traffickers' phone numbers, but they also showed tremendous diligence in the onerous task of listening to the wiretaps.[8] As Hafer recalled, "By the time the case was over, those guys

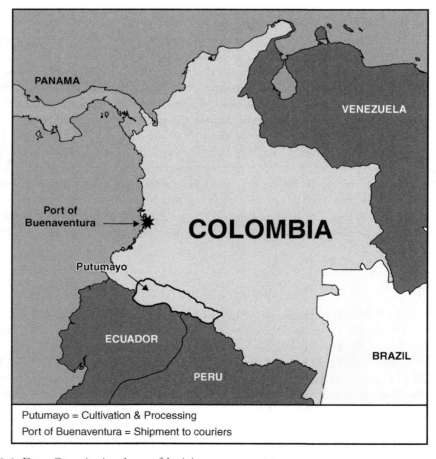

FIGURE 12.1 Drug Organization Areas of Activity

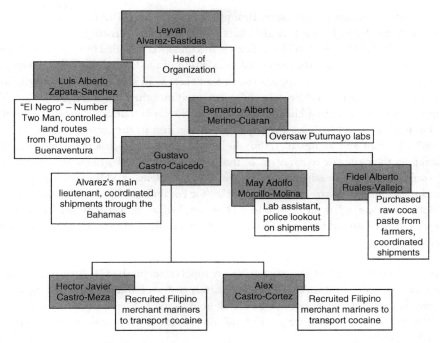

FIGURE 12.2 Organizational Chart

[the Colombian officers] spent thousands of hours—literally—listening to wiretaps. Their cooperation was key, because the calls were mostly in Spanish and almost always in some kind of code."

Sorting through all of the recordings—and hearing endless thinly veiled references to cocaine shipments as "skirts" or "girls"—the Colombian officers working the wiretaps began to piece together the structure and membership of the trafficking organization, which controlled everything from production to distribution. Several members of the group oversaw cultivation and processing of the coca crop itself in the southern jungle region of Putumayo, Colombia; others transported the processed cocaine; and still more recruited international mariners as couriers for cocaine shipments from the port of Buenaventura.[9] Figure 12.1 shows the areas where the organization's activities took place.

Along with extensive undercover work done by UC-1, who made over 50 trips to Colombia during the investigation, the wiretaps also allowed the DEA and Colombian law enforcement to assemble a de facto organizational chart (see Figure 12.2).

The Effects Principle

Hafer and the DEA were sure that most of the cocaine was destined for the United States, which, as the largest consumer of the drug, accounted for 36 percent of the $88 billion market for cocaine worldwide.[10] But to gain a conviction, the team had to obtain evidence that the targets of the investigation knew that they were sending their drugs to the United States. Under customary international law, countries could criminalize activity that occurred entirely outside of their borders in one of several

86 Chapter 12

circumstances.[11] Most relevant to Operation Beanpot was the "Effects Principle," which allows nations to prosecute acts "intended to have substantial effect within the state's territory."[12] Congress invoked this principle in passing 21 USC § 959, which explicitly states that it "is intended to reach acts of manufacture or distribution committed outside the territorial jurisdiction of the United States."[13] However, to satisfy the Effects Principle, § 959 limits its application to traffickers who ship drugs "*intending ... or knowing* that such substance or chemical will be unlawfully imported into the United States."[14]

Hafer's only option for bringing charges against the Colombian traffickers, most of whom never set foot in the United States and had no other criminal connection to the country, was to use 21 USC § 959 and § 963 (Attempt and conspiracy); thus, he needed solid proof that the narco-traffickers knew they were shipping their cocaine to America, or intended to do so. Under the statute, proof of intent or knowledge could be provided exclusively by circumstantial evidence, and there was ample circumstantial proof in this case, given the size of the U.S. market for cocaine and the destinations of the vessels on which the defendants smuggled their cocaine.[15] However, Hafer—and specifically his superiors in the U.S. Attorney's Office—wanted hard proof that the defendants planned to send the drugs to America. As Hafer explained:

> The first real pushback I had was convincing my supervisors [in the U.S. Attorney's Office] that we should actually [pursue] this case. The problem was that everything on the wiretaps was in code. Everyone knows Colombian cocaine nearly all goes to the U.S., and I told my supervisors, "I can prove this to a jury." But until we got that call, they were very skeptical that we should charge the case in Massachusetts.

The Big Break

In March 2008, the team finally intercepted a call that could establish where the suspects intended to send the drugs. After months of listening to wiretaps, the Colombian DAS officers assigned to Operation Beanpot monitored a call from the cell phone of Hector Javier Castro-Meza, a member of the Alvarez-Bastidas operation who recruited mariners to transport drugs, to a satellite phone on board the *Malaga*, a large container ship. Castro-Meza's conversation with a Filipino merchant mariner (later known as "Cooperating Witness #3," or CW-3) on board the vessel was brief, but supplied the magic words—in a rare phone call in English—that the investigators had been waiting for:

CW-3: The trip was cancelled. We are not going to the "N."
Castro-Meza: You no go to New Orleans? You no go to New Orleans? Wait, you no go to New Orleans?

Hearing "New Orleans" (repeated six times in all) was exactly what Hafer needed for prosecution under 21 USC § 959. The recording provided clear evidence that Castro-Meza knew the drugs were intended for the United States; other defendants in the case also referred to this shipment, proving that they too knew that the drugs were destined for New Orleans.

The March 2008 intercepted phone call not only gave Hafer solid proof of the traffickers' knowledge that their drugs were being shipped to the United States, but also provided Barton's DEA squad with a new target and potential source of information: the Filipino merchant mariner who was smuggling drugs for Castro-Meza on board MSC *Malaga*. The team wanted to interview CW-3, but in order to do so,

MSC *Malaga* would have to land in the United States, or failing that, the DEA would need cooperation from the country in which the *Malaga* made port. Following the ship was easy; all of its ports of call were public knowledge. But unfortunately the ship was not destined for the United States, but rather for a host of foreign countries where either the DEA did not have good relationships with local law enforcement (such as Pakistan) or countries with which the United States had bad relations generally (such as Syria and Iran). Without local connections, the DEA squad was powerless to do anything other than wait for the wiretaps to elicit further information.

The Romanian Connection

Eventually, over a year later, MSC *Malaga* added a new port of call: Constanta, Romania. Unlike her previous stops in unfriendly nations, this port call was in a country that had an excellent working relationship with the DEA. Although the DEA did not have an official field office in Romania, agents based in Athens and Sofia had worked with the Romanian Border Police on other cases with great success.

The Operation Beanpot squad knew that this was their best chance to interview the merchant mariner who had called Castro-Meza. Special Agent Grella took the lead on this assignment, since he had experience with cases involving Filipino merchant mariners from his prior posting in Singapore. Grella and two other agents flew to Romania immediately—an arduous three-flight trip that took nearly twenty-four hours. Arriving in the port city of Constanta, Grella and his team were feted by their Romanian colleagues, who were so excited by the opportunity to work with the DEA that they hosted a huge welcome dinner for their American guests.

The next day, April 14, 2009, MSC *Malaga* docked in Constanta. Not wanting to tip off the other mariners to the DEA's investigation, Grella needed the help of Romanian authorities to disguise the DEA presence. At the request of the DEA, the Romanian Border Police staged a large-scale, lawful immigration sweep of the ship to allow Grella to interrogate CW-3 without drawing attention to him. Romanian police pulled each of the fifty or so sailors off the boat for individual interviews. When it was CW-3's turn, however, the interviewers included not only Romanian police, but also Grella.

Grella told CW-3 what he knew about his smuggling activities, his planned trip to New Orleans, and how the DEA tracked him to Romania. After hearing what the DEA already knew, CW-3 quickly decided to cooperate. As Hafer explained:

> I can't even imagine what was going through this guy's mind. He's in the middle of nowhere, in a port in Romania, and some American agents come and grab him off a ship. It was like something out of a movie. But [CW-3] had no criminal record before this, and I think he knew that cooperating was his best chance.

CW-3 filled in more details on how the narco-traffickers recruited merchant mariners to move their drugs out of Colombia. In CW-3's case, members of the organization had first approached him during his shore leave in Buenaventura, Colombia, in December 2007. On his first port call, "Ali" (defendant Alex Castro-Cortes) bought him drinks. On his return visit to the country a month later, Ali met him again and paid for his visit to a local brothel.[16] Afterwards, Ali and "the boss" (defendant Gustavo Castro-Caicedo) asked if he wanted to work for them as a courier: for moving a ten-kilogram package of cocaine into the United States, the traffickers would pay him $3,500 per kilo.[17] CW-3 accepted, and later received the cocaine package on MSC *Malaga* from a Colombian stevedore. As for the drop-off location

88 Chapter 12

for the cocaine transaction, the traffickers' connections in the United States were so extensive that he was told, "any of the [half-dozen] scheduled port stops in the United States were fine."[18]

With CW-3's information and ongoing cooperation secured—including a requirement that he testify at a future trial of the traffickers—the DEA let him go. He got back on board MSC *Malaga* like all the other sailors whom the Romanian police had temporarily detained. True to his word, he kept Grella's team apprised of his whereabouts and contacts with the traffickers in Colombia, and even forwarded several emails he received from them.

With CW-3's cooperation, Grella and Hafer were hoping to seize a "live load" cocaine shipment, including recordings of the phone calls setting it up. Once again, however, progress of the investigation hinged on international cooperation and the varying laws of host countries. While CW-3 consented to a voluntary recording of his phone calls, agents also had to ensure that local laws permitted such recordings.[19] When MSC *Malaga* took CW-3 back to the Philippines, a country that forbids one-party consent for recorded conversations, Grella had to wait for several months for CW-3 to land in ports of call in countries where such recordings were allowed. The *Malaga* was planning to stop in Hong Kong, where one-party consent recordings were legitimate, but, frustratingly, the *Malaga* changed her itinerary and never went there.

Nonetheless, CW-3 confirmed the key piece of evidence that Grella, Barton, and Hafer needed: the traffickers intended to send their cocaine to the United States via the port of New Orleans. Combining CW-3's testimony with hours of damning wiretaps, the Operation Beanpot team believed that they possessed enough solid evidence to obtain a conviction. It was time to indict the case.

Indictment and Extradition

Back in Boston, Hafer brought the case before a federal grand jury in July 2009. The indictment was short and simple, running barely three pages, and charged eight defendants with conspiracy to violate the narcotics importation statutes under 21 USC § 963.[20] Once the jury returned a "true bill," the defendants were indicted and the prosecution officially began. None of this information, however, was public. The indictment was placed under seal while Hafer and Barton worked on the next step: having the defendants arrested in Colombia.

Under the terms of the United States' extradition treaty with Colombia (as with many other nations),[21] the first step in any extradition proceeding is the preparation of a "provisional arrest warrant" (PAW) for each defendant.[22] Each PAW contains an affidavit from the prosecutor and the lead agent on the case, as well as significant background information about the proof the government has of the defendant's guilt. The affidavits must be sworn in front of a U.S. magistrate, then sent to the U.S. Embassy in Bogotá for an official translation into Spanish. The PAWs are then given to a Colombian judge, who certifies them, allowing Colombian law enforcement to arrest the defendants.

Preparing the nearly 100 pages of affidavits was only one hurdle; getting the Colombian justice system to act on them was another matter entirely. Here again, however, the long-standing relationship between U.S. and Colombian law enforcement was critical. As Hafer recalled:

> Even at this stage, when we had to go through all of the formal bureaucratic steps, having a good relationship with the Colombian authorities absolutely expedited things and moved the process along. Otherwise—if it weren't for the good relationships that our judicial attachés had created in Colombia—our paperwork could have sat there for months.

Instead, in just over a month, the PAWs were approved and members of the vetted DAS and CNP units were ready to make arrests. Once again, Colombian law enforcement performed admirably and arrested all eight indicted defendants in simultaneous raids in September 2009. The DAS and CNP officers proved their continued dedication to Operation Beanpot, as well as demonstrating considerable creativity in how they carried out the arrests. The Colombian officers were worried about one defendant in particular, Luis Alberto Zapata-Sanchez (El Negro), who had a reputation for violence. DAS devised a creative plan to capture him without tipping off the remaining seven defendants. Instead of arriving at Zapata-Sanchez's remote mountain plantation in Colombian police vehicles and wearing police uniforms, DAS agents posed as members of the United Self-Defense Forces of Colombia (AUC), a right-wing paramilitary organization. The DAS officers rappelled into Zapata-Sanchez's compound from Blackhawk helicopters and whisked him away under the guise of an AUC "kidnapping." Unwilling to admit that the "AUC" had scored a victory, Sanchez's men did not alert any of his co-conspirators, who were all arrested by the CNP shortly afterwards.

Once the eight indicted defendants were in custody in Colombia, Hafer had to secure their extradition to the United States. Despite the provisional arrests, extradition was by no means guaranteed—it still required judicial approval, and the signature of Colombia's then-president Alvaro Uribe. As part of the extradition treaty, the DEA had to make various assurances to the government of Colombia, including that the United States would not seek the death penalty or life imprisonment for the defendants. But beyond those formal requirements, Hafer simply needed the president's office to act on his extradition request—soon.

While the official extradition treaty made the subsequent prosecutions legally possible, what actually brought the defendants to the United States were, once again, the good working relationships established with Colombian law enforcement and judicial officials. Immediately after submitting the formal paperwork, the Department of Justice's judicial attachés at the U.S. Embassy in Colombia started pressing for extradition. In the meantime, the eight indicted defendants were housed in a special prison, both to ensure their safety and avoid corruption. The CNP also arrested twelve more individuals who took part in the narco-trafficking conspiracy. Those defendants, who were not slated for extradition to the United States, were placed in regular Colombian jails. Colombian officials, including the vetted CNP and DAS officers staffing the case, pleaded with Hafer to seek extradition of these individuals as well, lest the corrupt Colombian judiciary let them slip away unpunished. Hafer understood the complexity of this issue:

> The Colombian [officers] were still thrilled about the case overall, but were disappointed that we couldn't extradite those twelve as well. Sometimes as a prosecutor, you have to make tough decisions. And if we're going to extradite people to the United States, we have to make sure we're getting the biggest fish, which I think we did in this case.

The Colombian officers' fears about the local courts proved well-founded: within a few weeks of their arrests, all twelve men had their cases mysteriously dismissed by Colombian judges.

Nine months after the provisional arrests—a lightning-fast time in the world of international prosecutions—President Uribe signed the extradition paperwork that allowed the defendants to be transported to the United States for trial. Now, however, the problem was venue. The venue provision of the U.S. Constitution generally requires that criminal trials "be held in the State where the said Crimes shall have been committed."[23] However, for crimes "not committed within any State, the Trials shall be

90 Chapter 12

at such Place or Places as the Congress may by law have directed."[24] In the case of 21 USC § 959, which explicitly covers "acts of manufacture or distribution committed outside the territorial jurisdiction of the United States," Congress directed that: "Any person who violates this section shall be tried in the United States district court at the point of entry where such person enters the United States, or in the United States District Court for the District of Colombia."

Hafer realized the potential legal complications in this seemingly simple provision. The small jets used by the U.S. Marshals Service to extradite prisoners could not fly nonstop from Bogotá to Boston. The logical refueling point would have been Miami, but Hafer had concerns:

> We had to be precise regarding the plane's itinerary not only to make sure we got venue in Massachusetts, but also because DOJ is not exempt from internal competition, and cases like that have, in the past, ended up in Miami.

The Marshals Service and its pilots next suggested the U.S. Navy base at Guantanamo Bay, Cuba. But given the murky legal status of Guantanamo Bay, Hafer also rejected that option. Finally, with another instance of international cooperation, this time from The Netherlands, the Marshals Service received permission for a refueling stop in Curaçao, a Dutch Caribbean island.

On July 22, 2010, the eight defendants from Operation Beanpot finally arrived in Boston. While the U.S. Attorney's Office in Boston was already publicly touting the success of the investigation,[25] Hafer knew that a great deal of work remained in order to secure convictions against the eight defendants, either by plea agreement or trial.

Prosecution

Although none of the defendants was willing to talk to the DEA or prosecutors while in Colombia, most of them changed their minds after extradition to the United States. Hafer was particularly interested in securing plea agreements and cooperating testimony from the two leaders of the trafficking organization, Leyvan Alvarez-Bastidas and Luis Alberto Zapata-Sanchez:

> Getting the main two [defendants] to plead was the big thing in my mind. If they pleaded guilty, I assumed that the others would follow. But it was a long process, with negotiations over nine to twelve months. They had high-priced and experienced extradition lawyers from Miami. In the end, I showed them how strong our case was, and even flew up the Colombian cops and let their lawyers interview them off the record.

Hafer's strategy eventually paid off. The two main defendants pleaded guilty in 2011, and five others followed suit shortly thereafter.[26]

One defendant, however, insisted on going to trial. Gustavo Castro-Caicedo was Alvarez's main lieutenant and the coordinator of shipments through the Bahamas. His main defense at trial would be to admit that he was involved with drugs in Colombia, but deny that he had any knowledge that the cocaine was destined for the United States. Hafer set out to build the strongest possible case proving that Castro-Caicedo knew the destination of the cocaine he shipped. In doing so, he relied heavily on the Colombian wiretap recordings and the continued help of the vetted DAS unit:

During the trial prep, I would run across a recording and think it was a good call that I could use at trial, but I'd need more background information about it. All I had to do was call the Colombian agents we worked with, and I'd have an answer back by email five minutes later. If you had to go through a formal process every time you needed this kind of information, it would never happen.

In addition to organizing and translating thousands of hours of cell phone recordings, Hafer also had to deal with pre-trial legal challenges from Castro-Caicedo. While many involved routine issues, such as the defense's motion to exclude any mention of his prior heroin trafficking conviction,[27] two other motions dealt specifically with the international nature of the case.

First, Castro-Caicedo challenged the legality of the indictment by claiming that the "Rule of Specialty" was violated. The Rule of Specialty "generally requires that an extradited defendant be tried for the crimes on which extradition has been granted and none other."[28] This requirement ensures that the terms of the extradition treaty,[29] which allow for extradition only for specified offenses, are not violated once the prisoner has been moved out of the country. Castro-Caicedo argued that the prosecutor's filing of "§ 851 information" ("Proceedings to establish prior convictions") about his prior heroin conviction— which would apply only for sentencing purposes after trial if convicted—violated the Rule of Specialty because it (partially) tied his punishment to an offense for which he was not extradited.[30] The government countered that the Rule of Specialty, by the plain language of the extradition treaty, only applies to the offense for which a defendant is tried, and that judges must always be able to consider a defendant's entire criminal history when determining an appropriate sentence.

Second, the defense argued that the Colombian wiretaps violated the Fourth Amendment. Specifically, Castro-Caicedo claimed that Operation Beanpot was a "joint venture" because U.S. law enforcement agents "controlled the Colombian investigation."[31] Therefore, the defendant's motion argued, the Fourth Amendment applied and wiretaps that were legal in Colombia were inadmissible in American courts because they were not approved pursuant to U.S. law. On this motion, the government argued that because Castro-Caicedo was not a U.S. citizen and the conversations were recorded outside the United States, the Fourth Amendment did not apply, per the Supreme Court's decision in *Verdugo-Urquidez*.[32]

Judge Mark Wolf, who was assigned the cases of all eight defendants, rejected both of Castro-Caicedo's motions and sided with the government's arguments in a hearing held on June 20, 2012.[33] On the defense's first claim, Judge Wolf concluded that the Rule of Specialty was satisfied in this case because Castro-Caicedo was prosecuted for an offense specifically covered by the U.S. extradition treaty with Colombia. On the second claim, the judge also ruled in favor of the government on the extraterritorial application of the Fourth Amendment. Judge Wolf noted that in order to raise a valid Fourth Amendment objection to foreign wiretaps a non-citizen defendant must show some "sufficient connection"[34] to the United States, which Castro-Caicedo lacked.

After almost six years of investigation, Castro-Caicedo's trial finally began on September 19, 2012. The trial was, for the most part, uneventful. It included testimony from several of Castro-Caicedo's co-conspirators, including the ringleader of the operation, Leyvan Alvarez-Bastidas. CW-3, the Filipino merchant mariner, also testified. But most striking was the testimony about the wiretaps from two Colombian law enforcement officers in the vetted DAS unit. In this final phase of Operation Beanpot, the Colombian officers were once again eager to cooperate. Ironically, however, Hafer had to deal with an international hurdle created not by the Colombians, but by the U.S. Department of Homeland Security (DHS): securing visas for the two Colombian officers. When Barton and Grella personally vouched for the two officers, DHS relented just in time for the trial.

92 Chapter 12

Castro-Caicedo himself declined to take the stand and testify. After six days of trial, on September 27, 2012, the government rested and sent the case to the jury. The jury deliberated for only a few hours before returning with a verdict: guilty. Hafer, Barton, Grella, and the entire DEA and DAS teams working on the case were satisfied: Operation Beanpot was officially a success.

Notes

1 Press Release, U.S. Attorney's Office for the District of Massachusetts, "Colombian President Approves Extradition," July 22, 2010, accessed July 2, 2015, www.justice.gov/usao/ma/news/2010/July/OperationBeanpotPressRelease. html, http://perma.cc/7TAV-J84E.

2 See, for example, United States Department of the Treasury, Financial Crimes Enforcement Network, "Black Market Peso Exchange Update," June 1999, accessed July 2, 2015, www.fincen.gov/news_room/rp /advisory/ html/advis12.html, http://perma.cc/C544-CWW8; Oriana Zill and Lowell Bergman, "The Black Peso Money Laundering System," *PBS Frontline*, accessed July 2, 2015, www.pbs.org/wgbh/pages/frontline/shows/drugs/ special/blackpeso.html, http://perma.cc/U9JJ-GUAK.

3 Ginger Thompson, U.S. Agents Launder Mexican Profits of Drug Cartels, *New York Times*, December 3, 2011, accessed July 2, 2015, www.nytimes.com/2011/12/04/world/americas/us-drug-agents-launder-profits-of-mexican-cartels.html?pagewanted=all, http://perma.cc/GH8X-SL8E; *SGS-92-X003 v. United States*, 74 Fed. Cl. 637, 646 (Fed. Cl. 2007) (describing AGEOs in an unrelated case).

4 Gov't Trial Brief at 2, *United States v. Castro-Caicedo*, No. 09-10216-MLW (D. Mass. July 17, 2012), ECF No. 157, 2012 WL 2995328.

5 Ibid., 3.

6 Drug Enforcement Administration, Foreign Offices: Andean & Southern Cone Region, accessed July 2, 2015, www.justice.gov/dea/divisions/international/andean.shtml, http://perma.cc/CTD4-M5Q5.

7 Jose De Cordoba, "Decorated Colombia General Pleads Guilty to Corruption," *Wall Street Journal*, August 20, 2012, accessed July 2, 2015, http://online.wsj.com/article/SB100008723963904444435045776017333056 94876.html. http://perma.cc/YAQ4-MWKG; "Corruption in Colombia: Closer and Closer to the Top," *The Economist*, July 29, 2011, accessed July 2, 2015, www.economist.com/blogs/americasview/2011/07/corruption-colombia, http://perma.cc/H67V-CGQS.

8 Transcript of Change of Plea at 38, *United States v. Alvarez-Bastidas et al.*, No. 09-10216-MLW (D. Mass. June 27, 2011), ECF No. 166.

9 Gov't Trial Brief at 3–4, *United States v. Castro-Caicedo*, No. 09-10216-MLW (D. Mass. July 17, 2012), ECF No. 157, 2012 WL 2995328.

10 United Nations Office on Drugs and Crime, *World Drug Report 86*, "Cocaine," 2010, accessed July 2, 2015, www. unodc.org/documents/data-and-analysis/tocta/4.Cocaine.pdf, http://perma.cc/4XD6-DT6H.

11 See RESTATEMENT (THIRD) OF FOREIGN RELATIONS § 402 (1986) (describing the bases for extra-territorial jurisdiction).

12 Ibid. at § 402 cmt. d.

13 21 USC § 959(c).

14 21 USC § 959(a) (emphasis added).

15 See, for example, *United States v. Hernandez*, 218 F.3d 58, 66 (1st Cir. 2000) ("Given the nature of the crime, '[k]nowledge and intent in narcotics cases often must be proved largely by circumstantial evidence,'" quoting *United States v. Valencia*, 907 F.2d 671, 678 (7th Cir. 1990)).

16 Gov't Opp. to Def.'s Motion to Suppress Identification Procedure at 1–3, *United States v. Castro-Caicedo*, No. 09-10216-MLW (D. Mass. Aug. 28, 2012), ECF No. 186, 2012 WL 3789342.

17 U.S. Attorney's Office for the District of Massachusetts, "Colombian President Approves Extradition."

18 Gov't Opp. to Def.'s Motion to Suppress Identification Procedure, 1–3.

19 See RESTATEMENT (THIRD) OF FOREIGN RELATIONS § 433(1)(b) (1986) (requiring consent and "compliance with the laws both of the United States and of the other state").

20 Indictment at 1–3, *United States v. Alvarez-Bastidas et al.*, No. 09–10216-MLW (D. Mass. July 22, 2009), ECF No. 2, 2009 WL 6690858.

21 See United Nations Model Treaty on Extradition, art. 9 (1998).

22 Extradition Treaty with the Republic of Colombia art. 11, US–Colom., Sept. 14, 1979, S. TREATY DOC. 97–8 (1981) (entered into force Mar. 4, 1982).

23 U.S. CONST. art. III, § 2, cl. 3.

24 Ibid.

25 U.S. Attorney's Office for the District of Massachusetts, "Colombian President Approves Extradition."

26 See Transcript of Change of Plea at 38, *United States v. Alvarez-Bastidas et al.*

27 Def. Motion in Limine at 1–3, *United States v. Castro-Caicedo*, No. 09–10216-MLW (D. Mass. July 13, 2012), ECF No. 151, 2012 WL 2995327.

28 *United States v. Saccoccia*, 58 F.3d 754, 766 (1st Cir. 1995).

29 Extradition Treaty with the Republic of Colombia, art. 15.

30 Gov't Opp. to Def. Motion to Dismiss the Indictment at 17, *United States v. Castro-Caicedo*, No. 09–10216-MLW (D. Mass. Jan. 27, 2012), ECF No. 124, 2012 WL 370222.

31 U.S. Opp. to Def.'s Motion to Suppress at 5, *United States v. Castro-Caicedo*, No. 09–10216-MLW (D. Mass. June 8, 2012), ECF No. 143, 2012 WL 2091928 (quoting Def.'s Motion at ¶¶10–14).

32 *United States v. Verdugo-Urquidez*, 494 US 259 (1990).

33 Order, *United States v. Castro-Caicedo*, No. 09–10216-MLW (D. Mass. June 20, 2012), ECF No. 145.

34 *Verdugo-Urquidez*, 494 US at 265.

13

TWO CRITICAL INGREDIENTS OF INTERNATIONAL COOPERATION

The "Colombian Connection" described the U.S. Drug Enforcement Agency (DEA) and the Colombian police working closely as a single team to round up a dangerous, well-financed, and politically connected group of transnational drug dealers. Together, the two nations used an informant and an undercover agent to "work with" the criminal enterprise on the final stage of the production process of international drug dealing: money laundering.

If this investigation took place in the United States it would be relatively straightforward. Roughly, the required steps are to either "turn" a member of the gang exchanging leniency for information; or else to convince the gang that a DEA agent is really a money launderer or in a position to provide some other essential assistance. On sufficient information from either source, wiretapping or placing a bug would become an alternative (or a supplement) to further human penetration of the organization to gather the information and, perhaps, the evidence necessary to identify and convict the members of the gang. In any case, the goal of the investigation is to be in a position to document for a jury the flow of drugs to customers in the United States or the flow of laundered money into havens safe from money laundering investigations and charges. These steps can be described in five stages.

In the first stage, since both the sale of drugs and the laundering of its proceeds are done in secret and produce no complaining witness, law enforcement has to be able to seek out invisible crimes. One obvious way, as the Colombian case illustrates, is to catch someone working with the group (often in one of its more visible roles) and threaten him with conviction and a long sentence unless he helps law enforcement to penetrate the secrecy surrounding the membership, financing, and activities of the group. What is clear is that law enforcement has to find a way to seek out otherwise invisible crimes and then begin to target them in the ways we have described.

A second stage is to prioritize potential investigations so that prompt and significant attention is given to the most promising cases and, inevitably, less attention goes to the multitude of less important crimes. Figures collected by students of Mexican crime indicate not only that a very large number of crimes are never reported to the police but also that a significant percentage of those reported are never investigated.

The third stage is to investigate. Different nations and different law enforcement bodies within a nation have different capacities—manpower, skills, and resources—for investigations. Legal authority is equally important. In the "Colombian Connection," Colombia had relatively relaxed standards for wire-tapping; the United States, relatively severe ones.

The fourth stage is prosecution. The evidence necessary to satisfy the criminal statutes may be satisfactory or not, depending on the statutes in a particular country or region. To charge the gang in the "Colombian Connection" in the United States, the investigators had to obtain evidence that the organization intended to sell its drugs in the United States, a difficult step in the circumstances of that case.

Finally, there must be a fact-finder who can be trusted to process the information produced by the prosecution fairly. If the judges are corrupt or intimidated, it may be of little significance how thorough the investigation is.

Each of these stages and steps are well within the capacity of the Drug Enforcement Agency and the federal prosecutors in the United States. The judicial process is generally fair. The statutes are comprehensive. The investigators are skilled and not generally short of legal and financial resources, including the authority to use electronic surveillance, informants, and undercover agents. Our federal prosecutors are very good compared to most countries. Our courts are honest and needn't fear punishment for an honest verdict, especially by a 12-person jury.

But what if much of the evidence and many of the suspects are in another country? How difficult does it become to carry out the five necessary stages?

The Effort to Use Extradition and Mutual Legal Assistance Treaties to Coordinate the Efforts of Two States

A victim state ("V") cannot, as we have seen, itself investigate within the borders of another haven state ("H") without the consent of state H, and this consent is rarely given except for a joint operation with the police of state H. At the same time, state H will not give a strong priority to assisting state V in its investigations, given the other demands on state H; so neither state V (which prioritizes an investigation located in state H but cannot investigate in state H itself), nor state H (which does not find V's concerns its highest priority), have both the legal authority and the political will to carry out the part of an investigation that takes place in state H. State V can carry out the part of that investigation which left traces in state V but that part is likely to be inadequate to convict the high-level suspects located in H. When H wants help, the situation is simply reversed.

The traditional remedy to this investigative stalemate has been the adoption of treaties under which V agrees to help H when evidence or a suspect H needs is in V; in exchange for H promising to help V when their needs and capacities are reversed. But, as we saw, despite such treaties these stages and the overall strategy are vastly more difficult to carry out when they take place in two countries having different interests and using two or more different organizations and systems of law. This is especially so in organized crime investigations and trials likely to require broad, intensive and swift cooperation between two states and where some of the crimes, some of the evidence, and some of the perpetrators are located in each of the countries. Even if there are only two states and they have promised each other, by treaty, to cooperate in furnishing evidence or extraditing suspects for the other, the mechanisms for this are politically unreliable and administratively slow and rigid.

96 Chapter 13

The difficulties of duplicating a wholly domestic investigation and trial by treaties of cooperation between two states such as V and H come in three forms.

First, the legal arrangements and social/political understandings needed for complicated, long-term, organized crime investigations may not be present. The resulting lack of speed and fluidity of responses when mutual legal assistance and extradition treaties are used can be fatal to an investigation where the results of each step are likely to suggest another step best taken promptly. If the first step involves significant delay during the application of an MLAT treaty, the second step, that will become useful only on the basis of what is learned from the first, may become useless or impractical over the period of delay. If every request for investigative assistance must go through an elaborate process in the requested state on the basis of a significant paper product prepared by the requesting state, steps that should be taken will be left out in the interest of speed or convenience or as a result of confusion.

A truly cooperative system would involve more than formal requests and formal responses to requests. As happened in the Colombian case, States V and H would jointly attempt to allocate each "next" step in an investigation either to state V or to state H depending on the comparative advantage each had in carrying out that step, based on legal authority, skills, resources, location, and much more. Some steps would be left for state V; others would be taken on by state H. Prosecution would take place wherever the evidence the investigators had jointly assembled could best be used.

Second, in general, only one of the states (V) is sufficiently concerned or affected by a crime to take responsibility for the investigation. Its requests to the other state (H) for assistance, based on reciprocal agreements to help, will only bear fruit if someone connects the parts of the criminal enterprise taking place in H to the gaps geography left in the evidence available to V. But H may not even know of the criminal organization worrying V, let alone be greatly concerned by the parts of its activities occurring in H. The system does not, for example, lead H to seek out crimes of planning if their victims are in state V and only their planning and profits are in state H. Seeking out such barely visible crimes involves a substantial investment of time and resources that will only be invested if there is a substantial concern by the state whose investigative resources are needed. This concern is often lacking.

The investigation will have to compete with a number of other possible uses of investigative resources in state H. The victims are in state V; so H is unlikely to give priority to V's request over investigations that more directly benefit state H. The requests by state V are also not likely to fit neatly into the investigative capacities of state H; so state H may not understand what steps are needed or may not have the skills to carry them out, even assuming they are authorized under the law of state H to do so. The availability of critical techniques such as electronic surveillance, the use of government undercover agents to facilitate what looks like criminal behavior, the recruiting and paying of informants, and the placing of witnesses in government protection may be available in V but not in H or vice versa.

Third, the prosecutors and investigators from state V may not trust the prosecutors and investigators from state H. If they don't, they will withhold evidence that can be helpful to state H both in the investigative and prosecutorial stage and forego requesting steps that require funneling sensitive information to H's authorities. In a later stage, if the individual is to be tried in state V, his extradition from state H has to be approved by H's judges and political figures who may feel much closer to the offender than to the victim. In the "Colombia Connection," the American prosecutors found it just short of miraculous that Colombia was able to extradite suspects from Colombia only nine months after the first requests from the United States were received. Those conspirators who were tried in Colombia wholly escaped justice.

The Magic Hidden Behind the Success of the "Colombian Connection"

The Colombian Connection was a masterful, coordinated investigation of a significant transnational organized crime group because it solved the three problems not addressed by familiar treaty arrangements: trust, common purpose, and needed institutional mechanisms.

Without trust in the honesty and determination of a partner agency in law enforcement, cooperation is crippled. In the Bulger case described in Chapter 9, an FBI agent, John Connolly, was relaying information about the FBI's investigation of Whitey Bulger's Winter Hill Gang to Whitey Bulger and his associates. That would make a surprise search or a secret wiretap impossible. Steps designed to have the many advantages for the government of being covert automatically become overt when even a single well-placed law enforcement agent is in fact a double-agent working for organized crime simultaneously. Because information that can reveal the sources and methods of one government's investigation puts lives at risk as well as rendering covert surveillance useless, intelligence will not be provided by one nation to another suspected of having been infiltrated.

Trust does not magically appear; it must be carefully cultivated. DEA and specially created and vetted Colombian law enforcement experts worked together for a decade—training and carrying out joint operations and, above all, building work-based colleagueship. Similar processes had developed trust between the United States and the Romanian authorities who, as a trusted third party, played a crucial role in the investigation.

The second requirement is a common purpose, or if you like, a common target or enemy. That is necessary if there are to be costly steps of cooperation by both countries and not just by the one that is more obviously or immediately threatened. In the Colombian Connection, Colombia saw the drug gang as a threat to its own interests sufficient to motivate and, with success, reward the Colombian law enforcement agents who, in alliance with the DEA, brought it down. Many, many hours were spent, for example, by Colombians monitoring the phone calls of members of the group. This could not have happened without a strong, common purpose; it could not have been motivated by a treaty obligation alone. Colombian investigators came to the United States as witnesses to U.S. trials. The motivation was not just friendship; it was a powerful desire to see the defendants legally convicted.

It is convenient to bundle into this second category a somewhat different ingredient that we have not yet mentioned. Even the law enforcement agencies of a single country (such as the FBI and the DEA in the United States) find it extremely difficult to cooperate against a common enemy unless the credit for a successful investigation and prosecution is shared. A common purpose is thus not quite enough by itself. It must be accompanied by shared credit—a requirement often furthered by bringing the foreign law enforcement officers to be honored in the United States or vice versa.

The third requirement is the easiest to meet. Even when trust, a common purpose and shared credit are all in place, there is still need for both sides to share understandings of the routines and mechanisms of cooperation. How will cross-nation communications and training be carried out in terms of language, legal culture, and technology? How will each side learn of the constraints or opportunities presented by the other side's law and politics? What standard operating procedures and other routines will characterize cooperative operations in terms of organization, transport, equipment, and resources? How are strategic decisions on targets, methods, and sequence of covert and overt steps to be made, and by whom? What will be the process for resolving disputes?

All three requirements were put in place consciously and patiently in the "Colombian Connection," creating a far more complete, fluid, and lasting scheme of cooperation than treaties alone can produce.

PART FOUR

Moving the Proceeds of Organized Crime in Secret

Introduction

When we contrasted the business of Starbucks selling coffee to the business of the Sinaloa Cartel selling cocaine, two crops grown and processed in Colombia, the requirements of a successful business for the legitimate commodity, coffee, were to grow, produce, and transport it from the south, Colombia, to a market in the United States, for example in Detroit. When the product had been sold in Detroit, the difficulties for Starbucks were substantially over. The proceeds could be placed in a bank and be used both to pay for those who had provided goods and services earlier in the process and to reward the managers and owners of Starbucks.

For an organized crime group the business of the enterprise is only half over when its representative receives the proceeds from wholesalers in Detroit. For U.S. sales a Latin American business in illicit drugs requires the northern movement of drugs to be followed by a southern movement of the proceeds, both of which are risky and of critical importance to the cartel's business. Once it obtains its proceeds by street sales in Detroit, Sinaloa still has the problem of moving these proceeds, which are subject to forfeiture and the movement of which constitutes a serious crime, southward and across borders to pay the producers, processors, smugglers, and transporters, and to reward the managers and owners of the business. Indeed it is not at all unusual for the second half of the business, the southward movement of cash to Latin America, to be carried out by independent contractors who are not employees of the cartel itself.

Those responsible for an ongoing organized crime smuggling enterprise include both of two teams. The "A" team produces, smuggles, transports, and contracts to sell the drug or other contraband by organizing a passage north from Colombian fields to Detroit streets. Then the "B" team needs to organize a movement of the cash proceeds south from a stash house in Detroit to those in the "A" group in Colombia, Guatemala, or Mexico who are promised a share of the proceeds.

Without having the proceeds of sales in Detroit to distribute among the "A" team, the business will collapse. The illegal drug business requires a northern movement of contraband, such as drugs, followed by an equally essential southern movement of the proceeds of sales. Because the enterprise will collapse if either half of the cycle is disrupted, law enforcement will attack both the movement of the drugs north and the movement south of the proceeds of sales in the United States. Preventing the flow of money south has been a less than successful effort. To assess why this is so and how it is carried out in the game of moves and countermoves against law enforcement, we will look at two separate causes.

First, there is the difficulty of defining fairly a criminal prohibition of hiding crime-based money—creating a prohibition that is both fair and effective in its application to each of a number of ways the cartel may seek to move money. The source of the difficulty is simple. While it is easy to prohibit helping a cartel dispose of its proceeds from a criminal business without incurring the suspicions of law enforcement, the steps taken require a further condition: respect for an American and capitalist tradition of allowing the sellers of goods and services to mind their own business as long as they do not "purposely" assist a crime. It is a deep tradition in the United States that businessmen are not responsible for the uses to which are put goods and services they make available to the general public on similar terms. It is not considered the fault of the businessman if a criminal customer wants to use the businessman's goods or services in his plans to hide the proceeds of the plan's success.

The second difficulty is related but more practical. Even with the best drafting of a statute forbidding money laundering, there is likely to be a multitude of false positives when either the owner of a legitimate business or a law enforcement agent tries to determine whether a particular customer intends to use the product of that business to transfer the proceeds or the means of crime. There may be a thousand transactions that give rise to some vague suspicion that the goods normally sold for legal purposes will be misused for criminal purposes. But only a handful of the thousand are likely to turn out to be either *purposeful* assistance in crime as an accomplice or *purposeful* money laundering. Determining which transactions actually are money laundering will be costly and time-consuming and saving effort, time, and money by presuming the transaction is not money laundering will allow the few occasions when it really is money laundering to accomplish the illicit purpose.

It is extremely important to an organized crime group that those who are involved in moving money proceeds, from a place where contraband was sold for that money, back to the entrepreneurs, suppliers, transporters, smugglers, and others who made it possible, be able to do that without revealing the history of these proceeds of crime. As we saw in the account of Operation Beanpot, knowing this history would be a very important source of evidence to law enforcement. Tracing the money physically or through accounts will identify: who "earned" these proceeds by crime in a city such as Detroit; who stored the proceeds pending transportation; and who, by his labors and skills at producing, smuggling, and transporting the contraband is owed money for having exercised those skills. Such information can be all that is needed to make a strong criminal case for illegal manufacturing and selling of drugs. It will also justify government forfeiting the proceeds or the instrumentalities of the crime and sale of drugs.

Obviously an organized crime group involved in selling contraband is as anxious to hide these facts as law enforcement is to discover them. We will examine in the next chapter the ways in which such evidence from the transfers and movements of money might be hidden from law enforcement by an organized crime group.

14

MOVING PROCEEDS OF CRIME WITHOUT REVEALING THEIR HISTORY

XYZ Cartel's Money Problem

As the chief financial officer (CFO) of XYZ Cartel, a drug trafficking organization based out of Mexico, you have a serious problem with how to handle all the incoming currency. The cartel brings in over $7 million per week which is sent to regional stash houses across the United States. You are responsible for determining how to move this money for the cartel, and your boss does not tolerate failure gracefully.

XYZ Cartel's books showed that about 80 percent of the drug revenues are used by the cartel for business expenses, primarily for three purposes: (1) bribing officials; (2) paying cartel employees; and (3) purchasing narcotics from suppliers. Thus 80 percent of revenue has to be put back into the business. The remaining 20 percent is profit, and you must also launder those funds so that when the time is right, the cartel bosses can retire in luxury. Additionally, you are responsible for developing a strategic reserve of funds so that the cartel won't miss payments or narcotics deliveries if a large police action were to disrupt some of the cartel's current operations.

Step 1: Bulk Cash Smuggling—Getting the Money Back into Mexico

The first problem facing you, as the CFO of XYZ Cartel, is getting most of the money back into Mexico. Drug trade revenues must be smuggled back across the border to pay for expenses. Like all businesses, XYZ Cartel has expenses which include, for a drug organization, paying suppliers for raw materials, bribing local officials, paying salaries, buying warehouses and vehicles, building cash reserves, etc. Since most of these expenses need to be paid outside of the United States, the cash allocated for paying them must be smuggled south. For Mexican drug trafficking organizations bulk cash smuggling is a prominent method for moving drug sales proceeds to fuel their business.

The (now defunct) National Drug Intelligence Center estimated that $17.2 billion was smuggled into Mexico in bulk cash shipments over a 2-year period spanning 2003 and 2004. Another estimate, utilizing a "ground up" extrapolation from analysis of individual cartels, put the figure more conservatively at about $3 billion annually. Considering additional estimates that $19 to $29 billion of annual cash flow

102 Chapter 14

from the U.S. to Mexico is needed to fuel the drug trade, we see that bulk cash shipments represent a significant portion of total drug trade revenues.

While money laundering is often associated with the *profits* of illicit activity, bulk currency smuggling (particularly in the U.S.–Mexican drug trade) is often associated with the *operational funds* of drug traffickers used for business expenses. Since this money is spent in the illicit supply chain where suppliers will not question the source of the funds, there is no need to hide the money's connection to criminal activity; however, this flow of currency still must be hidden from authorities.

With the increased "dollarization" of Latin American economies, once the money is physically transported out of the United States, the cartels are often able to make use of these funds directly for illicit business transactions, without undergoing the additional scrutiny that may have resulted from converting these large sums of dollars into various other currencies.

The simplest way to get the funds south has been to have the money transported across the U.S.–Mexico border. Not only is this uncomplicated, but it's also highly unlikely to be detected by authorities. The ways in which currency can be smuggled are nearly limitless, from cargo containers, to private jets, to teddy bears. That said, with the expansive and porous nature of the U.S.–Mexico border, most currency smuggling into Mexico takes a less sensational form, being hidden in vehicles or carried by individuals.

An additional technique entails using daily border crossers to carry small amounts of money (usually between $5,000 and $10,000) from the U.S. into Mexico. This reduces the batches of smuggled money below customs reporting requirements and decreases the impact of any singular interdiction at the border.

While cash transportation is typically managed by members of a Mexican cartel, an outsourcing model is often also available, managed by independent contractors or brokers. This outsourcing reduces the logistical burden on cartels of creating their own smuggling network, but comes at an increased cost to move the money.

Interestingly, the increase in bulk cash smuggling can also be seen as a natural response to increasing anti-money laundering (AML) efforts in the banking system. As AML pressure ramped up after the attacks of September 11, 2001, criminals turned to moving larger amounts of money via bulk cash smuggling to avoid the increased vigilance exercised by financial institutions and law enforcement.

In sum, as CFO of XYZ cartel you are likely to direct that a significant portion of the proceeds of the sale of the cartel's drugs first be taken to counting houses and converted to larger denomination bills. From there, you have them sealed and vacuum packed to reduce their size. Finally, you arrange for drivers, pilots and crewmen on boats to conceal the packages in hidden compartments in cars, trucks, planes, and boats to transfer physically across the border to a second set of safe-houses where the money can be recovered and used for operations.

Step 2: Structured Deposits—Placing Funds Into the U.S. Banking System

Even with an expansive smuggling operation, you still have a large quantity of dollars not being smuggled across the border. Ideally, this money would be placed inside banks so XYZ Cartel could enjoy all the benefits of modern banking; placing illegal proceeds into the banking system increases flexibility in how you can use the funds. Once the money is in the banking system it also becomes much easier to conduct layering through banking services, from wire transfers to using certificates of deposit as collateral to secure loans.

Unfortunately for you as CFO, U.S. regulations dictate that many transactions (including cash deposits) greater than $10,000 require financial institutions to file reports reviewable by financial institutions' analysts and law enforcement personnel—a scrutiny best avoided by the XYZ Cartel.

One well-established technique for defeating these reporting requirements is to structure transactions below the reporting thresholds. This is commonly referred to as "smurfing" and entails breaking deposits, transfers, or withdrawals into multiple smaller transactions, under the $10,000 reporting requirement. By spreading the transactions among numerous banks and accounts, it is possible to move hundreds of thousands of dollars a day without crossing reporting thresholds. XYZ Cartel pays individuals to take the cartel's funds, and then deposit them into various bank accounts and across different bank branches. In this way, suspicion regarding the deposits is minimized.

XYZ Cartel can easily move $600,000 per week ($120,000 per work day) of funds in this manner, constituting the majority of the cash remaining in the United States after the bulk cash smuggling into Mexico. (We will explore what XYZ does with the remaining $400,000 per week below.) Although this appears to be an impressive sum of money that would be hard to disguise, with just 25 bank accounts, XYZ Cartel can stay below the $10,000 reporting threshold, even if only depositing funds into each account every other day ($4,800/account if depositing every day, $9,600/account if every other day). Furthermore, by varying the amount of funds deposited in each account, the deposits can appear more natural and less associated with a laundering scheme. The individuals depositing the money (referred to as "smurfs") are paid between 0.5 percent and 1.5 percent of the money deposited, a small fee for you to get the money into the banking structure.

Once money is deposited inside accounts, it can also be "churned"—transferred back and forth between accounts to further complicate paper trails. Combining churning and the commingling of illicit proceeds with legitimate funds (from business fronts, see more below) makes it challenging for investigators to determine which or how much of the funds associated with the account are tied to illicit activity.

Step 3: Business Fronts—Placing Funds Into the U.S. Banking System

Even after the structured deposits, you still have $400,000 per week of remaining money in the United States. Since you as CFO understand the value of diversifying the methods of placing funds into the banking structure (to make it more difficult for law enforcement to track and less of an impact if law enforcement halts one form of laundering), you want an alternative method to move funds into the formal banking channels.

For this you utilize cash-intensive businesses (business receiving a high proportion of their sales revenue in physical currency) to disguise illicit funds from crime as the proceeds of legitimate sales. Cash-intensive businesses not only simplify this commingling, they also decrease the chances of auditing officials uncovering anything incriminating. Since the operation of business fronts is in violation of the Money Laundering Control Act (discussed further below), this is a worthwhile precaution for you to take.

In this scheme, the launderer inflates the sales of a business by claiming that some illicit funds were actually the result of sales from the business front. Large laundering operations utilize multiple business locations, such as the numerous New York City pizzerias used in the historical and long-running "Pizza Connection" case in the mid-1980s. These cartel-run establishments also do not have to be overly concerned with making a profit since they are supported by infusions of illicit funds, and can survive even when legitimate business is poor.

104 Chapter 14

XYZ Cartel rents out storefronts, giving instructions to its members on the basic steps required to run a legitimate pizzeria or bar, including the hiring of employees, purchase of inventories, and basic accounting. On top of any legitimate sales made, they also forge receipts to provide a false paper trail indicating that illicit funds channeled through the business resulted from legal sales. Being particularly careful, the operators will even purchase enough raw materials (e.g., pizza dough, liquor) to ensure that the cost-side of the business matches reported sales. This further protects the operation from audits by the authorities.

The cost of laundering money in this manner is roughly the expense of the purchases of the raw materials as a percentage of the commingled sales figures. Thus, the incentive is to launder in industries with particularly high margins, and in this case that is why you as CFO got involved in pizzerias and bars, two simple business models with high margins.

You open 50 establishments around the nation, using each location to produce fraudulent receipts of $8,000 per week. This provides XYZ Cartel with a method for laundering $400,000 per week into the formal banking channels, with business records to back up the legitimacy of the funds.

These business fronts can also be used to provide a criminal associate with a "legitimate" salary, which can reduce suspicions of unexplained wealth and serve as a method to integrate funds. Cartel members claiming to be managers of the front business can get paid a wage commensurate for the position providing a plausible explanation for their income.

To further obfuscate ownership of these funds, the proceeds of these businesses can be funneled into shell corporations, entities used to disguise the true ownership of assets. These shell corporations have no purpose beyond laundering and are not used to conduct any other legitimate business. By layering multiple shell corporations on top of one another (i.e., having shell corporations act as the owners of other shell corporations), or placing them in different jurisdictions such as offshore tax havens with strong privacy laws, it can become very difficult for authorities to determine the true owners and directors of the shells.

These shell corporations are created fairly easily through filing a few documents, including many that can be completed over the Internet. Although most jurisdictions require a local agent to reside within the country, there are local (and in XYZ Cartel's case, unscrupulous) attorneys and others who are willing, for a fee, to act as agents for the shells. Bank accounts can then be opened underneath the shells, hiding the true ownership of the accounts and their assets, as in the widely publicized case of the Panamanian law firm, Mossack Fonseca.

Once the money is in the shell accounts, it can then be layered by funneling it through different shell corporations in different jurisdictions. Obtaining the records from each different state will generally require what we have seen is a quite slow mutual legal assistance request. Because each successive request depends on the results from the previous one, this process can take years. If the shells are incorporated in countries with strict secrecy laws, it will be still more challenging for authorities to determine true ownership. Even if they can, it is easy to register the shells under nominees, intermediate agents who participate in transactions on behalf of the launderer, but who have no genuine interest in the transactions.

Offshore accounts in jurisdictions with strong privacy laws can be a dead end for investigations and provide a haven to launderers. In these cases authorities can only look to international organizations, such as the Financial Action Task Force (described below), to pressure these havens to reform their banking regulations.

Step 4: Trade-based Laundering—Layering and Integrating Illicit Funds

Through structured deposits and business fronts you are now placing $1 million per week of XYZ Cartel's funds into the formal banking sector, but with additional layering transactions, you can make it even harder for investigators to uncover the true origin of the placed funds. Additionally, if cartel leaders want to utilize the cartel's profits for personal reasons, they need a way to make the money available to them.

Through purchasing and selling intentionally over- or undervalued merchandise—known as trade-based laundering—value can be moved between parties, financial institutions, and nations while creating the appearance of legitimate business transactions. Although this seems similar to the business fronts discussed above, this form of laundering involves transactions *between* business entities, rather than the accounting of revenue within a single business.

By misrepresenting the price of goods being bought and sold by organizations, value can be transferred between colluding buyers and sellers. The organization buying goods for less than they are worth *gains* value; they end up in possession of goods worth more than they paid for them. The organizations selling goods for less than they are worth *lose* the same amount of value. This results in a transfer of value to the underpaying buyer from the seller. The reverse transaction, moving value to the seller from the buyer overpaying, is also possible.

These transactions can be used to move value across borders, or legitimatize large sums of money through seemingly authentic business transactions. With most customs agencies inspecting less than 5 percent of cargo shipments, this misrepresentation of value poses a very low risk of detection, and even if inspected, it is often difficult, if not impossible, to determine the true value of the goods.

To make this alternative means of moving funds available to the cartel leaders, as chief financial officer you might establish an important export company for each senior member of the cartel; using shell corporations you set up earlier, you arrange for large quantities of expensive merchandise (let us say, gold watches) to be purchased on the open market. This step transfers the value of the cash from narcotics sales into these watches. The shell corporations then sell the watches to the import-export companies at a cost of $10, much reduced from the market value of $1000 at which you purchased them. This step transfers the value of the watches to the import-export company. The import-export companies then sell those watches abroad at slightly below market price to ensure a quick sale, in this case $750. The inflated spread between the cost of the watches and the price at which they are sold—$740 per watch—is an apparently legitimate profit for the import-export company that is put into an account for the cartel leader. These import-export companies can be established nearly anywhere in the world, allowing cartel leadership to decide where to keep the proceeds of their illicit activities.

With global merchandise trade over $16.7 trillion dollars a year, the ability for authorities to screen these transactions for fraudulent invoicing is limited. A study analyzing import-export data for suspiciously high and low prices found that in 2004, $167 billion flowed out of the United States in overpricing of imports and underpricing of exports, while $223 billion flowed into the United States from underpricing imports and overpricing exports. These are massive flows of value that, while certainly not all tied to money laundering, demonstrate the magnitude of the opportunity for trade pricing manipulation and the potential for hiding transfers of value in that channel.

Certain goods in various markets have prices that defy economic realities which may indicate to the authorities the existence of trade-based money laundering. However, prosecutions for this type of

106 Chapter 14

activity have been virtually non-existent, and you as CFO of XYZ Cartel can rest comfortably in the knowledge that authorities will not be able to effectively respond to this method of laundering.

Step 5: IVTS—Placing Funds Abroad and Layering Them Into the U.S. System

XYZ Cartel also has many expenses outside of Mexico. For some of these expenses, particularly cocaine purchased in Colombia, it is more efficient to move the money directly from the United States to suppliers in Colombia, without first smuggling the money into Mexico. This can be accomplished by moving money through informal value transfer services (IVTS), which are transnational financial networks that function outside the formal banking system.

A typical IVTS exchange involves four parties, an individual in Country S (Sender) who wants to send money to an individual in Country R (Recipient), as well as an agent in Country S (Agent S) and an agent in Country R (Agent R). To send the money, the Sender provides the cash to the agent in her country, Agent S. Agent S then provides the Sender a code to collect the money in Country R, as well as informing Agent R details about the amount of value being transferred and the collection code. Meanwhile, the Sender provides the Recipient in Country R the collection code. The Recipient then goes to Agent R in Country R, provides the collection code and collects money equal to the transferred value.

Since Agent S is receiving money and Agent R is distributing it, eventually Agent S and Agent R must balance their accounts. This is done either through reverse IVTS transactions from Country R to Country S, or through other value transfers from Agent S to Agent R via check, wire transfer, physical transfer of cash, money orders, etc.

Through the use of an IVTS, you can send funds directly to Colombia. Such a relatively well-established (thanks to narcotics trafficking) illicit IVTS to Colombia is referred to as a Black Market Peso Exchange. In this IVTS, you give dollars to a representative of the exchanger in the United States. The exchanger finds businesses in Colombia that need U.S. dollars to purchase supplies in the United States. The exchanger connects the two counterparties, places the U.S. dollars into accounts for use by the Colombian companies and puts the Colombian pesos into an account for use by XYZ Cartel. In this way, no money moves across borders where it can either be intercepted at the border or traced through electronic funds transfer records kept by banks and other financial institutions. The exchanger takes a share of the transaction, typically between 20 percent and 25 percent (legitimate IVTS services charge 2 percent or less). XYZ Cartel can then use the funds in Colombia to pay for its raw supplies of cocaine.

Greater attention has been given to money laundering through IVTS since the attacks of 9/11 due to the putative association of IVTS to terrorist financing. However, many systems for IVTS emerged primarily as an inexpensive method for migrants and short-term workers to transfer money to remote locations. These systems are often culturally embedded and are very common throughout much of Eurasia, including China, Hong Kong, India, the Philippines, Thailand, and the Middle East. For those without access to formal banking, IVTS may often be the only available channel for remittances.

Using Another's Laundering Machine

Operational aspects of an international criminal organization such as XYZ Cartel demand flexibility in its uses of cash. To remain adaptable to changing customer demands, law enforcement actions, and competition from other cartels, XYZ Cartel needs a way to quickly manipulate the location of laundered funds. By utilizing the laundering systems of other organized criminal enterprises, funds can be laundered to and from almost anywhere for a premium fee, reaching up to 30 percent.

The Russian mafia has a presence along Mexico's west coast, particularly in hotels and casinos; the Russians will take money either outside or inside of Mexico, and provide laundered funds back to the cartel in the United States, Mexico, or in any country convenient for the cartel. This significantly reduces the burden on XYZ Cartel for having laundering networks capable of immediate adaptation beyond their standard practices. Using the Russian system allows XYZ Cartel to focus on its core laundering activity without developing an overly robust network that accounts for a wide range of contingencies.

The methods of money laundering we have just described are intended to disguise the source of funds placed in banks and investments or spent in cash for business or pleasure. But, as we shall describe in the last chapter, technology constantly changes the context and capacity for hiding evidence and surveillance of activities. Virtual currencies will not have to use banks or cash for most transfers of value; its owners and recipients will be almost unidentifiable; its transactions untraceable. Money laundering will become laundering of almost undiscoverable records. The to and fro of this aspect of organized crime will change.

15

THE LIMITED EFFECTIVENESS OF A BARRAGE OF PROHIBITIONS OF MONEY LAUNDERING

Introduction

We have already noted that following the trails and traces of the proceeds of crimes proves to be a very useful investigative technique for law enforcement. (Conceptually, the street seller of drugs would be followed as he received the proceeds of drug sales and carried them to a local stash house. After that the movement of the proceeds would be monitored physically or electronically until they reached and incriminated the leaders of an organized crime group abroad.) Seizing the proceeds or instrumentalities of crime also proves to be a useful supplement to a criminal prosecution as a deterrent.

After law enforcement started to take seriously both of these strategies, organized crime saw the necessity of hiding those valuable forms of evidence and abating the risk of seizure. Indeed, for an organized crime group to be a lasting business enterprise, the business must find ways not only to generate proceeds from illegal activities but also to make the proceeds safely available for use where they are needed or "owned." This requires secret forms of money laundering such as those described in the previous chapter.

In response to those secret forms, law enforcement developed a rich variety of statutes and regulations prohibiting what amounts to a cover-up phase of criminal business—a phase focused on secret or disguised transfers or deposits of the proceeds of crime. Some of these new rules addressed only financial institutions; others were broader. Some of these took the form of defining as crimes actions intended to hide the connection between money and its illegal sources; others took the form of mandatory banking regulations, generally promulgated by FinCEN, a division of the Treasury Department.

Whether these new laws were likely to be a useful response to money laundering depended on what use law enforcement hoped to make of them. The new laws could have been wanted to increase the punishment for the underlying crime or criminal business. But we have other simpler ways to attach aggravating factors to criminal statutes or to simply increase the penalty.

The new laws could instead have been intended to deter the bosses of an organized crime group from themselves engaging in a cover-up by hiding the traces of the money they had illegally earned. But it is almost impossible to imagine any person seriously engaged in crime who would continue to commit the crime, but refrain from hiding the evidence of it—thereby increasing measurably the risk of being caught—just to avoid a prosecution for money laundering.

The most plausible purpose was a third possibility: to deter the assistance of third-party facilitators in helping to cover up the underlying crimes. For an ongoing criminal business, those who can help dispose of evidence of past crimes are almost as critically important as those who plan and execute the next stages. Even if we are thinking of a single bank robbery, the useful steps by law enforcement to prevent or deter that type of crime include those that help to prevent a successful cover-up. Money laundering laws and regulations with this third purpose resemble in various ways being an accessory after the fact, or having subsidiary roles in carrying out a conspiracy, an obstruction of justice, or the New York crime of criminal facilitation.

Thus, in an early stage of the moves and countermoves of money laundering, organized crime learned to hide the movement and storage of the proceeds of its crimes from law enforcement agents and to place the proceeds more safely in secret places. In response, in a new stage, law enforcement began to develop a system of regulations to make hiding the trails of proceeds of crime far more difficult.

The Regulatory Regime

The Bank Secrecy Act (BSA) of 1970 provides the foundation. It requires currency transaction reports (CTRs) to be submitted to Treasury's Financial Crimes Enforcement Network (FinCEN) to prevent the placement and then secret movements of large amounts of currency into and then through a banking system or other financial institution. The financial institution is required, whenever a transaction in currency of over ten thousand dollars takes place, to file a report which can then be used by the Treasury Department in supporting enforcement actions or in discovering and publicizing the newest ways organized crime is laundering money. The 1970 Act also requires another report to be filed with FinCEN reporting physical transportation of monetary instruments in an aggregate exceeding ten thousand dollars into or out of the United States.

Under the BSA the Treasury Department further requires banks and other financial institutions to file a "suspicious activity report" (SAR) for any suspicious transaction relevant to a possible violation of statutes or regulations. Generally a financial transaction is regarded as suspicious if parts of it make no sense to the financial institution or appear to be done only for the purpose of hiding the transaction. The BSA also promulgated "Know Your Customer" rules, requiring financial institutions to collect information such as the name, birthdate, address, and taxpayer identification number for all customers and to verify the information about new accounts.

The BSA did not operate alone. Foreign financial institutions are only subject to their own laws and law enforcement, not to U.S. laws and law enforcement such as the BSA. To remedy the possibilities for evasion this leaves, in 1989 a number of western nations formed the Financial Action Task Force (FATF) to set standards and promote effective and uniform implementation of legal, regulatory, and operational measures for combating money laundering. FATF is a group policy-making body which also attempts to generate the necessary political will to bring about and then monitor national legislative and regulatory reforms in these areas. It is best known for developing in 1990 a series of recommendations that are recognized as the international standards for combating money laundering.

110 Chapter 15

Finally, in the late 1980s, Congress passed criminal statutes with sentences as long as twenty years for those who conduct a financial transaction:

> knowing that the transaction is designed in whole or in part either to conceal the nature, source, ownership, or control of the proceeds of a specified unlawful activity or to avoid a transaction reporting requirement under state or federal law. (These penalties were in addition to those for failing to properly file CTRs and SARs.)

In sum, for decades now there has been a system of regulatory reports, a system of international cooperation, and a system of criminal statutes all designed to use the assistance of financial and other institutions to prevent money laundering. Financial transactions of more than ten thousand dollars must be reported to FinCEN who will relay that information to law enforcement as well as explore what can be learned from the reports about new forms of crime and money laundering. Information provided in Suspicious Activity Report forms allows FinCEN to alert law enforcement and to identify emerging patterns of money laundering.

The Advantages of a Regulatory Regime Requiring Private Reporting Rather Than Relying Exclusively on Investigations by Law Enforcement

As sources of information needed by law enforcement, private participants in financial or commercial markets have several advantages over law enforcement officers. Familiar with normal transactions, they can and will spot minor irregularities or oddities in a transaction that are more likely to arouse their suspicion than the suspicion of outsiders. Dealing with many similar transactions and communicating with others in the business they can identify new patterns of activity as new forms of money laundering become fashionable. They can provide important leads to the investigators trying to turn a suspect into a defendant. Finally, there are vastly more private participants in financial and commercial markets than there are law enforcement agents; so the private participants are able to give vastly more attention to unconfirmed but troublesome suspicions than could ever be expected of law enforcement.

The Difficulties of Relying Exclusively on Criminal Statutes

Title 18 U.S.C section 1956 is the primary (and severe) criminal statute prohibiting money laundering. As we have noted, it forbids an individual to conduct a financial transaction:

> knowing that the transaction is designed in whole or in part either to conceal the nature, source, ownership or control of the proceeds of the specified unlawful activity or to avoid a transaction requirement under state or federal law.

The writers of the statute did not have to require the defendant to "know" that the transaction was designed to conceal the source of the proceeds of a specified unlawful activity. But, many would regard a prohibition of not exercising reasonable care to avoid unknowingly facilitating money laundering as too severe and too demanding. It would mean that, whenever a banker was foolishly trusting about the source of a deposit or a businessman was too trusting as to the assistance a fairly normal sales transaction could provide to laundering the proceeds of a crime, the banker or the businessman would be guilty of a crime carrying a very serious sentence (twenty years). "Knowing" protects the innocently mistaken and the negligent facilitator from a penalty far too severe for an unintentional crime.

However, a requirement of showing that a facilitator "knows" the source of money he was paid in a commercial or banking transaction is exceedingly difficult for law enforcement to satisfy. Organized crime has too many ways to keep facilitators (or to pretend to keep facilitators) from having the knowledge. It can disguise the cash proceeds of drug sales within the proceeds of legal businesses depositing huge amounts of cash. Casinos and supermarkets would be examples. It can divide the proceeds of crime into amounts considerably less than the ten thousand dollars required for a report by a financial institution and deposit those lesser amounts without reports into a number of bank accounts, later to be combined or spent. If the use of fractions of the amount required to come under the currency transaction report requirements is discovered it will be treated as money laundering, but new forms using multiple banks throughout the nation are very difficult to spot.

Organized crime can limit its activities in the FATF environment. It can hide laundered cash across borders in nations less effective in carrying out, or less committed to, the FATF structure or keep the money completely outside of the regulated financial system. Organized crime can, as we have seen, use the cash proceeds of drug trafficking to buy expensive goods from a foreign country—one that will not report the use of cash—and then sell the goods in a third state with the proceeds going to a drug cartel or other organized crime group. Looking to the future, organized crime may turn its stores of dollars into the form of a virtual currency which is not subject to the Treasury regulations and not subject to monitoring by the Treasury.

These transactions, too, are unlikely to be "known" to be illegal money laundering by those whose banks or businesses are secretly used to facilitate money laundering. A financial institution or a business person may or may not vaguely *suspect* money laundering in one of these transactions, but he or she can hardly *know* the illegal source of the funds.

The Present and Future of Money Laundering

An assessment of the present state of the contest of moves and countermoves in the strategic area of money laundering now favors organized crime internationally and in the United States. The United Nations Office on Drugs and Crime estimates that criminals, especially drug traffickers, may have laundered around 1.6 trillion dollars or 2.7 percent of global GDP in 2009—a figure consistent with the range previously established by the International Monetary Fund to estimate the scale of money laundering. Of this, less than one percent of global illicit financial flows are currently being seized and frozen.

The system of Treasury regulation, particularly the requirement for financial institutions to file suspicious activity reports, does not yet accomplish either of its two primary purposes: to permit law enforcement to know when and with what target to begin a major money laundering investigation and criminal case; and to permit FinCEN to identify emerging trends and patterns associated with financial crimes.

The set of international conventions, statutes and reporting regulations available to U.S. law enforcement have not proved very successful in stopping the flow of money across borders. The total amount seized by the U.S. customs and border protection in the two years after March 2009 was just one half of one percent of the estimated total of bulk cash shipments. Three major reasons for failure are obvious.

One cause of failure is a disinterest in inspecting what is moving *out* of a country *into* another country. In 2009/2010 customs officials inspected less than four percent of southbound traffic at the U.S.–Mexico border. A second part of the problem is that smugglers are for the moment technologically

112 Chapter 15

and strategically sophisticated; they have learned to use advanced communications equipment and methodology to avoid alerted check points.

A third major reason for failure is the inherent advantage of those who hide goods or cash moving across a border that is flooded with very large numbers of very large trucks carrying very large cargos every day. To find money crossing the border between the United States and Mexico requires an extremely time-consuming effort to search through the cargo and the truck carrying it. The cost is high in terms of both dollars and delay of the truck being inspected and those lined up behind it.

The problem of stopping money laundering becomes even more difficult if the form of the money laundering transaction were for the facilitator of money laundering to buy goods from China for dollars—goods that could then be sold in Mexico or Colombia for local currencies. Only a costly investigation would be likely to discover the stratagem. And yet such a transaction is also one of a multitude taking place every day between the United States and Mexico.

The Next Response of Law Enforcement

If the secret movement of money by organized crime groups is to be slowed, suspicious activity reporting needs to be broadened and more vigorously enforced beyond financial institutions. Law enforcement needs the help of people who are expert in a particular type of transaction to detect minor and suspicious peculiarities in such transactions, and to help with the very costly effort to determine who initiated the transaction, what he does for a living, and how it relates to his dealing with the businessman through whom the transaction might be laundered—a set of tasks far more difficult than searching a large truck.

What law enforcement needs most is the cooperation required in transactions with businessmen who are not bankers or other financial institutions. The businessman through whom a transaction in which goods purchased with laundered money are sold can best be detected using the assistance of a very large number of business men and women who can detect irregularities or unusual complexities of the transaction and report them to the government which can then pursue an investigation. This is the very function of suspicious activity reports now required to be filed by banks with FinCEN.

What is missing is a far broader insistence that non-financial institutions also file suspicious action reports based on current information about money laundering collected by FinCEN and its international counterparts. Virtual currencies may be the next move of organized crime in laundering money. Spreading the requirements of suspicious transaction reports will be the next countermove of law enforcement.

Suspicious activity reports used in this way would efficiently supplement investigative efforts by law enforcement to prove that particular facilitators had knowledge of the illegal source of the funds. At the stage of identifying suspicious transactions hidden in a multitude of legitimate ones, it will be far more effective to rely on a very large number of legitimate businesses familiar with the customs and routines of the business. It is only at the next stage—the investigation of the facts about identified suspects—that government investigators rather than private businessmen should take over.

The punishment for failing to report a suspicious transaction to government agents, who might then prove that it was in fact a step in a money laundering plan, does not deserve the severity that should be reserved for those facilitators who know they're assisting in money laundering. The next step of prosecuting the shipment of money south from the United States to drug producing and transporting states, such as Mexico and Colombia, is likely to be drafting the assistance of large numbers of business persons not directly involved in financial institutions. Organized crime's response simply is likely to be a move to virtual currencies where contact with business persons need take place rarely, if at all.

PART FIVE

The Future of Organized Crime

Introduction

In Part One we discussed three special problems of conducting a business dependent on behavior forbidden by law: (A) the threats of legal punishment posed by a state's law enforcement; (B) the resulting fact that the daily cooperation among participants must be carried out in secrecy, without open communications or records and without the help of familiar institutions, such as banks, or the assistance of social and legal demands for compliance with widely accepted rules of behavior; and (C) the threats of lethal violence posed by rival groups competing for illegal business. The organized crime group generally succeeds only if its costs of overcoming these difficulties are less than the benefits of selling one or both of two central product lines: either a relatively widely desired but legally forbidden good or service (a business in contraband which lacks the profit-reducing competition common to legal markets) *or* protection from a threat the organized crime group itself created and posed: extortion.

We have tried to show that, while some part of the business strategy of organized crime naturally duplicates the strategies of legitimate businesses, much of the strategy of an organized crime group flows from efforts to meet these three special conditions of survival. The choice of product lines that have willing or fearful customers reduces the availability of victims who are likely to give law enforcement notice of the crimes being committed. Laundering the proceeds of criminal activity effectively closes another source of critical evidence. The extensive use of corruption of law enforcement officers or higher officials creates and ensures a far safer environment for a group's activities. So does a practice of, and reputation for, using gang members to intimidate or eliminate victims and witnesses without whose testimony it may be impossible to convict those who have been arrested and await trial.

Alternatively, the organized crime business can deal with the threats of law enforcement by operating across borders for the advantages of leaving much of the critical evidence in a "haven" state with no great interest in discovering and prosecuting those activities occurring within its borders that harm only citizens of some other "victim" state. As to the threat of violent competitors, an alliance with corrupted police or with a particularly violent organized crime group or street gang may be necessary, feasible, and adequate to meet the threat (but at some significant cost).

114 Part V

United States law enforcement has, as we have seen, responded to the "moves" of organized crime with countermoves of its own: new crimes; new methods of surveillance or investigation; new reporting requirements; and new, specialized structures of prosecutors and police. Countries have responded with treaties and multilateral agreements aimed at expediting evidence gathering and exchange in transnational cases. More effectively, they have collaborated informally on investigations in the interest of several countries.

The fundamentals of these strategies of moves and countermoves will remain in the decades ahead. But much may change as a result of new technology, changes in the product line to reflect changed demand, and new strategies for dealing with the three inherent threats to organized crime groups. We begin Part Five with a review of the immense relevance of new technology in the contest we have described. The subject is what the Internet has already meant for the contest. Then, in concluding, we identify and consider eight moves by organized crime that may have a great effect on the set of concerns organized crime poses for states; and the countermoves law enforcement may adopt.

16

THE INTERNET AND THE EXPLOITATION OF THE "FOG OF WAR"

In previous chapters, we have seen that, historically, organized crime groups have profited principally from extortion and monopolizing the distribution of contraband—both goods and services. To avoid the fate of common criminals, they have protected themselves from prosecution by emphasizing "victimless" crimes that do not generate complainants (or extortion of those too frightened to complain) and by corrupting police charged with investigating those crimes. We have seen that law enforcement can successfully gather evidence against organized crime groups by seizing their records and conducting electronic surveillance of their meetings and telephone calls. But, as these groups have begun to operate transnationally, the ability to seize records and conduct electronic surveillance is stymied by law enforcement's severely constrained authority to conduct investigations across national borders and by the diverging interests of cooperating states.

The Internet has opened to organized crime groups new, highly profitable, transnational criminal activities. It has created new means for the groups to protect themselves from successful prosecution; it has even further impaired law enforcement's ability to collect evidence of their business activities and intercept their communications. Transnational organized crime groups that take advantage of the Internet can be the most difficult of all to investigate. The following hypothetical example illustrates the challenges in fighting organized criminals that use the Internet to commit crimes.

Sup3rman84's father, an army officer, made sure his son went to a university to become economically successful and politically well-connected. While a student, Sup3rman84, who likes to "hack" into other computer systems for fun, interacted online in cybercafés with other like-minded hackers, including m00ver and Th3dwArf.

One warm summer night, Sup3rman84 saw that Th3dwArf was online. He pinged Th3dwArf on ICQ, an instant messaging platform, and asked for Th3dwArf's help. Sup3rman84 was inside Hi-Tech, an American high-tech company's firewall, but was having trouble "mapping" the connections between computers and figuring out what information of value each of the computers stores.

116 Chapter 16

New Criminal Businesses Made Possible by the Internet

By exploiting the Internet, organized crime can extend the reach of many of its traditional activities internationally. It can:

(1) sell opioids such as Oxycontin without prescription over the Internet, rather than sell bags of heroin on the street;
(2) distribute contraband child pornography electronically, rather than from the backrooms of local storefronts;
(3) extort businesses by threatening to take down their computer networks and websites if they do not make protection payments, rather than by threatening to burn down the buildings in which the businesses are housed; and
(4) operate Internet gambling sites, rather than maintain gambling dens such as the Chinatown den we saw in Chapter 8.

The Internet also brings with it new business opportunities in a safer business environment. Organized criminal groups can now enter the highly profitable business of data theft, a business whose value eclipses that of hijacking tractor trailers full of cigarettes or alcohol. For example, groups can steal databases containing millions of saleable credit and debit card numbers; trade secrets pertaining to the development and manufacturing of state-of-the-art products; or sensitive military and government information from inadequately secured computer systems. Without the irreducible risks of hand-to-hand transactions, they can then sell the stolen information over the Internet highly profitably and substantially anonymously— be it to governments, state-controlled entities, terrorists, or simply fraudsters.

At this point, Sup3rman84 and Th3dwArf have a well-established relationship, even though they have never met each other in person, never talked to each other over the telephone, and cannot even be really sure in which country the other lives. The two had met online and found that their interests, technical skills, and resources were complementary. Sometimes Th3dwArf assisted Sup3rman84; sometimes Sup3rman84 assisted Th3dwArf. A cautious trust had grown between the two and both had profited from the relationship.

As a rule, after they hacked inside a computer system, they carefully worked their way toward the files with the most restricted access, be they computer-aided designs or financial records. Their experience had shown that restricted files were the most valuable. Once they had access to the files, either Sup3rman84 or Th3dwArf would copy them and sell them. According to their loose agreement, whoever "owned" the victim company's computer system (i.e., whoever had originally hacked into the system) was the one who had license to sell the stolen information.

Sup3rman84 and Th3dwArf each had an extensive network of online and physical-world associates on whom they could draw for specialized assistance with an unfamiliar aspect of a computer system or selling the system's spoils. Over time, their networks of associates coalesced, and associates had begun to refer to the group as "The Enterprise." Bound by a modern-day "omerta," The Enterprise never claimed or acknowledged that it had broken into a victim company's computer system. If an associate broke that rule, he was cut off from The Enterprise and lost his share of profits.

Obstacles to Investigations of Internet Crimes

Organized crime groups, as we have seen, favor victimless crimes, because without complainants they are likely to remain secret from law enforcement. Gambling, prostitution and drug sales are not reported

The "Fog of War" **117**

because none of the participants in those crimes has an interest in doing so. By entering the business of electronic crime, organized crime groups gain a new form of secrecy: their victims may not even recognize they are victims of crime. When an organized crime group steals a tractor trailer load of cigarettes, its owner knows something (large) is missing. The true owner and the organized crime group cannot both believe for long that they possess the same load of cigarettes simultaneously. When a group steals individuals' banking and credit card information, a corporation's trade secrets, or a state's confidences, it makes an electronic copy. The organized crime group leaves behind the original data and information, while it walks off with its equally valuable copy. At the least, the theft may not be recognized or reported for some time; at the most, the theft may never be identified as a theft.

A victim may first become aware that something has been taken when the copy is used or appears somewhere else, but even then there are generally viable alternative explanations for how the information or data was obtained. Rather than flowing from a computer breach, state secrets may have leaked through a person who had access to them, as it did in the WikiLeaks and Snowden cases. In another example, the ideas that underlie proprietary intellectual property may have been developed in parallel with another company, or simply be less secret and unique than was thought. Credit card and financial information is used in hundreds of places and may have been stolen from any one of them. The absence of plain evidence of data thefts not only often makes it exceptionally hard to limit the number of potential perpetrators, but also makes it hard to tell whether a crime has been committed at all.

Even when the victim suspects that a crime has been committed, transnational organized crime groups do not need to corrupt public officials to limit the likelihood or extent of a criminal investigation. Institutional and governmental victims often have strong incentives to limit law enforcement's involvement. Companies fear that if they publicly admit to having been the victim of an intrusion, they will lose customers who are afraid that their credit and debit card information is not secure with the company. Governmental institutions fear embarrassing themselves with voters by admitting that sensitive, confidential information was inadequately secured.

Consider just one example: the Albert Gonzalez case. In 2009, Albert Gonzalez pled guilty to stealing over 40 million debit and credit card numbers from nine companies. Filings before the Security and Exchange Commission reflected that, before his arrest, about half of those companies had not identified his intrusion into their networks. Of those that did acknowledge the intrusions, only a fraction acknowledged in their filings that credit and debit cards had been stolen; most acknowledged only that there had been an intrusion and that card numbers had been exposed, but they were uncertain how many had been taken.

Later that winter, Hi-Tech's president receives a call from one of his salesmen. They lost a major, long-time European client. The client is sorry, but these are difficult times for businesses and the client needs to carefully manage its costs. A new company from one of the former Soviet Republics is able to supply a production monitor that meets substantially the same specifications as Hi-Tech's monitor for 25 percent less cost. The salesman assumes the monitor was developed by some of the engineers that lost their subsidized work when the Soviet Union broke up and is manufactured at a fraction of the cost because of their lower wages.

Dubious, the president hires a firm to do a thorough internal investigation. The firm finds signs that the company's computer system could have been compromised. There is no way to be certain, however, because the logs created by the company's computer system are incomplete to begin with and are overwritten every three months if they are not needed. With the secret design of one of the company's major products perhaps stolen, the president turns to the FBI for help.

The rival production monitor is being sold by a company headquartered in struggling Uzbekistan. After a preliminary investigation, the FBI determines that the victim's corporate firewall logs do not reflect any connections to

118 Chapter 16

Uzbekistan. However, they do show inexplicable network connections to IP addresses in Yemen and Mongolia over the past several months. The logs don't capture what information, if any, was transmitted during these connections. The FBI further determines that one of the company's system administrators with broad access privileges was fired for poor performance during the pertinent period.

FBI investigators find that, during the fall, a cyber-informant for the French Police Nationale reported to his Parisian handler that Sup3rman84 was supposed to have some valuable design schematics for sale. When specifically asked, he said he had no reason to believe the schematics had been stolen from a French company or that Sup3rman84 spoke French.

Problems of Evidence Collection in Transnational Electronic Crimes

As with traditional organized criminal activities, during the first stage of the investigation of an Internet-based crime, investigators must narrow the group of potential suspects, generally to those with an opportunity and a motivation to commit the crime. With an Internet crime, the motivation—profit—may not narrow the field. And, unlike other forms of organized criminal activity, geography and physical access rarely constrain the pool of potential suspects. Literally, anyone in the world with access to a computer could have committed the crime.

Still, investigators can ask questions whose answers may prove helpful to narrow the pool of suspects in some cases. Who had the opportunity to commit the crime? Do computer forensics show that the network was accessed in a way that could have occurred only from certain physical locations? Did the crime require specialized knowledge of software or network design that was somehow limited to certain individuals or groups? Is it possible to identify where the stolen information or data was transmitted from and to? If so, can those locations be associated with a particular individual or group? Have similar tools or techniques been used elsewhere, that is, is there an identifying modus operandi? Where is the stolen information being sold or used? Can we work back from there? Lastly, is there useful cyber-informant information? Each of these evidentiary inquiries has its physical-world counterpart. How effective they prove to be in solving an Internet-based crime will depend on the circumstances and nature of the crime itself.

As crimes are committed internationally through cyberspace, key facts naturally get diffused among multiple jurisdictions. Even without an organized crime group taking affirmative steps to conceal its tracks, when a theft of financial information or data is initiated from one country, sent to computers in a second country, with intent that the information or data be sold in a third country, there are three national jurisdictions in which fragile electronic evidence relating to a crime may be found. Except for cases of terrorism, there is little sharing of investigative information among competitive law enforcement agencies in the area of cybercrime, even within the United States. This means that leads which lie in one agency's files rarely make it to another agency's investigation. Identification and sharing of investigative information is even less likely when it is held by law enforcement agencies in two different countries. Finally, it is likely that one of those countries secretly benefits from the theft of the other state's private or secret information.

In the physical world, moving across national borders creates vulnerabilities for organized crime. Organized criminal groups must establish a means of transporting contraband over long distances. They must build trusted networks within their own country—where they are likely to share a common community, have established corrupt relationships, and have means of physically disciplining individuals who

The "Fog of War" **119**

challenge their organization. They must also be able to establish the same security and control in distant countries.

Internet crimes are different. By moving transnationally, organized crime groups impede access to the traces of their electronic criminal activity and reduce the likelihood that they will be discovered. While transnational organized crime groups move freely and anonymously across electronic borders, law enforcement agencies must stop at those borders and seek the assistance of their counterparts abroad. Thus, while organized crime groups work literally at the speed of light, the law enforcement agencies tracking them are limited to the very sluggish speed of comity or of mutual legal assistance treaty requests. Evidence of an electronic crime often disappears long before traditional mechanisms for the exchange of evidence between countries can be effective.

The FBI does its best to follow up on what leads it has. With the cooperation of prosecutors, it subpoenas the fired system administrator's bank and charge account records. There have been no unusual deposits to his bank accounts and he has not traveled abroad.

The FBI is still waiting to hear back from Uzbekistan. The FBI legal attaché reports that Uzbekistan is developing a tradition of strongly safeguarding the privacy of its citizens. Formally, the laws prohibit access to bank records without a strong predication. Informally, the government is supported by the country's new entrepreneurial class and sees the United States as trying unfairly to preserve its historical technological advantage.

The FBI determines that the IP address in Yemen turns out to belong to an anonymous proxy server widely used by hackers to hide their trails on the Internet.

Of the various foreign law enforcement agencies, Mongolian national police, who have been trained at Quantico by the FBI, are the quickest to offer informal assistance. The IP address in Mongolia is assigned to a computer at a company in Ulaanbaatar that had been hacked. On the Mongolian computer is an encrypted portion of the hard drive which neither the Mongolian police nor the FBI has been able to decrypt.

The Limits of International Cooperation

Internet service providers, data storage locations, banks, software companies, and outsourcing companies can all be operating outside the victim state controlling the evidence investigators want to collect. Their ability and willingness to provide evidence in an investigation is affected by forces wholly outside the victim's and victim state's control. External politics can affect the speed or expansiveness with which a country in possession of electronic evidence is willing to provide it in response to a victim state request. For example, for a significant period Canadian law enforcement was slow in providing assistance to the United States after a highly publicized forced rendition of a Canadian citizen in which the United States was complicit.

In addition, a country that holds evidence may simply be slow to respond out of a lack of interest or resources. When no one within the foreign country has been victimized, there is little urgency to provide assistance. Russia and China each have been notoriously slow in providing assistance in collecting evidence against their own nationals when the victims of those nationals have been exclusively outside of their borders.

The collection of evidence abroad also can be affected by different laws. What may be routinely available by subpoena in the United States, for example, may require a court order or higher evidentiary predicate in a foreign country. Finally, a company in a foreign country possessing evidence of a crime may simply take advantage of its home court advantage—its knowledge of the players and its connections

120 Chapter 16

within the government—if it doesn't want to be cooperative. It may also discourage its government from providing informal, investigative assistance.

With evidence spread across several continents, with law enforcement stopped at the borders, and with several forces intentionally slowing the collection of evidence from third parties, organized crime may have little to fear when it moves transnationally to commit electronic crimes. What little there is to fear is being further reduced by technology available to organized crime. Law enforcement often cannot rely on the monitoring of communications, of the sort we saw in Chapter 8 in the downfall of Mao and his organization in Chinatown. The Internet not only permits individuals to engage in near-anonymous communication, it also allows communication between them in encrypted forms that are unbreakable as a practical matter. It also permits them to store records in encrypted form, preventing the kind of successful searches for records which further undermine brick-and-mortar crime groups like Mao's gambling den.

17

CONCLUSION

Predicting the Future of the Contest Between Nations and Sizable Criminal Enterprises

The Effects of Adopting New Products, Alliances, and Technology

New Products

The products sold by organized crime will continue to be chosen for both profitability and safety against observation and investigation by law enforcement, but there is no reason why they should continue to be the same drugs or drugs at all or the same forms of extortion. Profitability depends on consumer demand or the ability to create a demand for "protection," on supply of the needed ingredients or manufacturing capacities, and the costs of smuggling. If any of these change dramatically, as one might, the nature of the business will change, creating new problems for both organized crime and law enforcement.

New competition will have the same effect as changes in demand. As the United States begins to legalize marijuana, the profitability of Mexican production drops sharply, shifting the search for profits to other illegal drugs. The supply of opioids and the price of heroin has fallen off as suppliers in China and India and new Internet distributors have entered the market. The strength of the demand for particular drugs also changes with fads and experience. Cocaine use has well passed its peak. Opioid pharmaceuticals have come to compete successfully with heroin sales.

Consumer demand satisfied by organized crime groups in the future need not even be for drugs so long as it is for something the illegality of which limits competition and allows monopoly profits. It could be a demand for weapons or migrant laborers. The result will be new dangers of discovery, which would then require new precautionary tactics of organized crime and new responses by American law enforcement. Similarly there will be new and dangerous forms of extortion, for example by blocking badly needed access to the Internet; or by encrypting data someone else needs; or by threatening to disclose hacked or stolen trade secrets or personal identity information. Like other weapons of extortion, control of data could also be used to disable rival groups in contests for customers, retailers and smuggling opportunities.

A shift in products need not be motivated by a change in consumer demand or in the dangers of production and transportation. New theories of business strategy (proposed by Professor Clayton

122 Chapter 17

Christensen of Harvard Business School) emphasize disruptive innovation by smaller competitors that begins with targeting the market for lower priced products that major competitors are ignoring as they focus on premium brands. Only later does the smaller competitor expand into more lucrative sales of fancier products. A shift to that strategy might lead an organized crime group back toward illegal gambling, perhaps using a virtual currency to compete with state lotteries by selling a greater expected payoff per dollar gambled, and a safe, albeit illegal, freedom from taxation of any winnings.

Creation of the institutions and knowledge necessary for use of the anonymous virtual currency would also diminish the ability of law enforcement to attack the money moving from sales in northern cities back toward the southern producers and transporters of the contraband.

New Alliances

Besides product changes, the contest between organized crime and law enforcement will be shaped in new ways by new organized crime alliances. They may be with other organized crime groups or with violent terrorist groups or with governments such as Russia. Similarly, organized crime will find new havens supported by different ethnic groups or government factions, creating a needed safety from informants and asserting the availability of recruits. An alliance with a new ethnic, national, professional, or class group could replenish a needed pool of recruits and informants or build political ties with those who might otherwise favor heightened law enforcement.

The great fear of U.S. law enforcement has been of an alliance between organized crime groups and violent terrorist groups. The law enforcement response to any such alliance might quickly be to add any such cooperating organized crime group to a list of terrorist groups subject to the terrorist "material support" statutes and to shift toward the war model from the law enforcement model of fighting organized crime. The effects of that would be to change sharply our methods of addressing organized crime. An Internet-based virtual alliance would also permit engaging the help of skilled individuals around the world for particular attacks.

Technological Changes

Dramatic new technology has grown in recent decades to respond to the fear of terrorism and to facilitate new forms of relations between business and its customers. Powerful encryption will enable an organized crime business to enjoy more of the benefits a legitimate business draws from an unencumbered ability to communicate to its business associates, reducing one of organized crime's three vulnerabilities: having to conduct business in secrecy, without books and records and without the helpful support of legal and social understandings. Communications will be more frequent, while still secret. Business will be conducted with encrypted records and books instead of regarding any records and books as extremely dangerous to create and hold. Encrypted orders will be given to confederates or placed with suppliers without revealing their identities or what is expected of them. With encrypted Internet communications to local managers, globalization of organized crime will be more feasible and there would be a wider choice of location for havens where specialized responsibilities may be carried out because they are tolerated by local governments.

The first response of law enforcement to encryption will be as in its contest with Apple, to attempt in a number of ways to penetrate the technology being used. Any success in that effort will pose major risks to organized crime groups. The more likely response in the longer run will be for law enforcement to turn from searching for written records to other forms of surveillance technology produced to monitor terrorism—drones, GPS devices, captured cell phones, facial recognition technologies—and begin to use these technologies against organized crime groups as well. Such new forms of surveillance enable monitoring of terrorists' location, communications, physiological changes, personal relationships, and much more. Authorization for its use could be expanded to include targeting organized crime.

The technology of transportation will greatly change the struggle between law enforcement and organized crime. Smuggling goods and cash across borders may become far easier and safer if they are carried by drones rather than by motor vehicles that must pass through limited border checkpoints on roads. Drones can take advantage of law enforcement's inability to monitor great stretches of contiguous airspace between a multitude of points of takeoffs and another multitude of places of landings, especially if the use of drones to carry packages of drugs or cash becomes common. It is far easier, although already immensely difficult, to effectively monitor authorized crossing points for great volumes of traffic.

Law enforcement could respond by acquiring for its purposes vast stores of data about individuals, collected for commercial purposes by Facebook or Google. Law enforcement already has the authority and the capacity to acquire masses of data that is made available by suspects to commercial third parties and to process it to reach conclusions about who is working with whom, when, where, and in what ways. This capacity has been focused on terrorist threats but can be shifted to organized crime, especially in the face of any signs of an alliance between an organized crime group and a terrorist group. For example, information about one's activities or associations collected by GPS or in the form of phone or credit card metadata can be stored indefinitely, processed with recently developed techniques of "big data," and transported easily and without cost. Law enforcement could use its skills with this technology to identify and regulate relationships between businesses providing drone transportation and their customers. Organized crime may use the same techniques to target individual customers, informants, law enforcement, recruits, and victims. Analytic techniques applied to big data will allow both sides to create very detailed and intimate portraits of almost everyone.

New Strategies of Organized Crime

Organized crime will build on the advantages of operating from haven countries into victim countries. Internet cooperation of gangs in providing assistance to organized crime in carrying out operations will become worldwide. Law enforcement will respond as it did in the Colombia case by slowly but steadily building close and trusted forms of cooperation through shared training against a common organized crime enemy.

New government strategies for following the sellers of drugs may make it no longer safe for organized crime to use "stash" houses to store cash receipts for eventual transfer by motor vehicle across the border with Mexico. But there are a number of alternative strategies for smuggling proceeds to which organized crime would move. The countermove of law enforcement would be to develop other regulatory or surveillance techniques to observe any new efforts at money laundering.

Moves and Countermoves

As long as there are highly profitable markets that are protected from competition by statutes making illegal the sale of a widely desired product, there will be organized crime and the set of concerns it generates. At least this will be so if the tradeoff between profits and danger remains attractive to both

124 Chapter 17

leaders and recruits. That is why organized crime is likely to remain a serious problem for any state which provides the opportunity for profits free of normal economic competition in order to discourage the use of legally prohibited contraband. Indeed, and more broadly, organized crime will remain an endemic problem for any society where corruption and intimidation can guarantee protection of an ongoing "business" against law enforcement.

Still, organized crime is likely to remain, for most states, a problem manageable by an intelligent, energetic, and non-corrupt law enforcement. Indeed, wise leaders of organized crime will prefer to remain "manageable" rather than find themselves at war with the state's military and intelligence forces. There is a third possibility: for organized crime to become closely tied in the pursuit of wealth to the civilian and military leaders of the state. This last strategic option is unlikely to be stable; it has produced only divided, weakened leadership in states from Guatemala to Nigeria.

New products may replace old products; new alliances, old ones. New technologies may help deal with the three major threats to any organized crime group: law enforcement; rival forms of organized crime; and the cumbersomeness of operating outside the law in a modern society. But the concerns raised by organized crime are likely to remain manageable by relatively normal law enforcement so long as corruption and intimidation are vigorously pursued.

BIBLIOGRAPHY

Personal Narratives

Kroger, John. *Convictions: A Prosecutor's Battles Against Mafia Killers, Drug Kingpins, and Enron Thieves.* New York: Farrar, Straus and Giroux, 2008.

Mazur, Robert. *The Infiltrator.* New York: Little, Brown, and Company, 2015.

Puccio, Thomas P. *In the Name of the Law: Confessions of a Trial Lawyer.* New York: W.W. Norton and Company, 1995.

Studies

Ainslie, Ricardo C. *The Fight to Save Juarez: Life in the Heart of Mexico's Drug War.* Austin, TX: University of Texas Press, 2013.

Allum, Felia. "Local Politics and Organized Crime," in *Defining and Defying Organized Crime,* edited by Felia Allum, Francesca Longo, Daniela Irrera, and Panos A. Kostakos. New York: Routledge, 2010.

Andreas, Peter and Nadelmann, Ethan. *Policing the Globe: Criminalization and Crime Control in International Relations.* New York: Oxford University Press, 2006.

Bowden, Charles. *Murder City: Ciudad Juarez and the Global Economy's New Killing Fields.* New York: Nation Books, 2010.

Bowden, Mark. *Killing Pablo: The Hunt for the World's Greatest Outlaw.* New York: Atlantic Monthly Press, 2001.

Campbell, Howard. *Drug War Zone: Front Line Dispatches from the Streets of El Paso and Juarez.* Austin, TX: University of Texas Press, 2009.

Dawisha, Karen. *Putin's Kleptocracy: Who Owns Russia?* New York: Simon and Schuster, 2014.

Fukumi, Sayaka. "The Yakuza and its Perceived Threat," in *Defining and Defying Organized Crime,* edited by Felia Allum, Francesca Longo, Daniela Irrera, and Panos A. Kostakos. New York: Routledge, 2010.

Glenny, Misha. *McMafia: A Journey Through the Global Criminal Underworld.* New York: Vintage Books, 2008.

Jacobs, James A. *Mobsters, Unions, and Feds: The Mafia and the American Labor Movement.* New York: NYU Press, 2006.

Ledeneva, Alena V. *How Russia Really Works: The Informal Practices that Shaped Post-Soviet Politics and Business.* Ithaca, NY: Cornell University Press, 2006.

Pieth, Mark and Aiolfi, Gemma, ed. *A Comparative Guide to Anti-Money Laundering: A Critical Analysis of Systems in Singapore, Switzerland, the UK, and the USA.* Northampton: Edward Elgar Publishing, 2004.

126 Bibliography

Rempel, William C. *At the Devil's Table: The Untold Story of the Insider Who Brought Down the Cali Cartel*. New York: Random House, 2011.

Reuter, Peter. "Drug Markets and Organized Crime," in *The Oxford Handbook of Organized Crime*, edited by Letizia Paoli. New York: Oxford University Press, 2014.

Rubio, Mauricio. "Colombia: Coexistence, Legal Confrontation, and War with Illegal Armed Groups," in *Dangerous Liaisons: Organized Crime and Political Finance in Latin America and Beyond*, edited by Kevin Casas-Zamora. Washington, DC: The Brookings Institution, 2013.

Saviano, Roberto. *ZeroZeroZero*. New York: Penguin Press, 2015.

Schwartz Jr., Frederick A.O. *Democracy in the Dark: The Seduction of Government Secrecy*. New York: The New Press, 2015.

Stiftung, Heinrich-Boll, ed. *Transnational Organized Crime: Analyses of a Global Challenge to Democracy*. Bielefeld: Transcript, 2013.

Stille, Alexander. *Excellent Cadavers: The Mafia and the Death of the First Italian Republic*. New York: Pantheon Books, 1995.

Varese, Federico. *Mafias on the Move: How Organized Crime Conquers New Territory*. Princeton, NJ: Princeton University Press, 2011.

INDEX

Note: Page numbers in *italics* denote figures.

Abdollah, Georges Ibrahim 78
accounting records of organized crime groups 34, 104,
  105; encrypted 122–123
Administrative Department of Security (DAS),
  Colombia 83–85, 86, 89, 90–91, 92
alliances 6, 10, 17, 19, 25, 28, 30, 32, 48, 97, 113, 122
Al-Qaeda 26
Alvarez-Bastidas, Leyvan *85*, 86, 90, 91
Angiulo, Jerry 31, 60, 61, 62, 64
Apple 122
asset forfeiture 46, 99
Atlanta Olympics 52
attaché relationships 79, 88, 89
Attorney General Exempt Operations (AGEO) 82, 83
AUC *see* United Self-Defense Forces of Colombia
  (AUC)
Avilés Pérez, Pedro 8

Bank Secrecy Act (1970, BSA) 109
banking system: business fronts 103–104, 105;
  structured deposits 102–103
Barton, Dennis 82, 83, 86, 88, 91, 92
big data 123
Black Market Peso Exchange 81–82, 106
books and records of organized crime groups 34, 104,
  105; encrypted 122–123
Boston 28–29, 31–32, 44, 56, 57, 59–69
Boston Globe 63, 67
bribery 8, 12, 31, 33, 34; *see also* corruption
Bulger, James "Whitey" 28–29, 31–32, 56, 57, 58, 59–
  60, 61–69, 97

bulk cash smuggling *see* cash smuggling
burden of proof 41, 49
Bush, George W. 27
business fronts 103–104
business strategies of organized crime groups 35–36
businesses of organized crime 1–2, 5, 17; detectable
  traces of 30–31, 40–41; new technology and 116,
  121–122

Calderón, Felipe 12, 33
Cali Cartel 25, 26, 29, 34, 83
Callahan, John 66
Camarena, Enrique 8
Canada 119
capture of governmental institutions 18, 21
Carrillo Fuentes, Amado 33
cash smuggling 101–102, 111–112, 123
cash-intensive businesses 103–104
Casper, Denise 69
Castro-Caicedo, Gustavo *85*, 87, 90–92
Castro-Cortes, Alex *85*, 87
Castro-Meza, Hector Javier *85*, 86, 87
Castucci, Richard 66
charging strategies 54–55
Cheney, Dick 27
Chicago 21, 34, 44, 56
child pornography 30, 116
Christensen, Clayton 121–122
CIA 25
Ciulla, Frank 61
CNP *see* Colombian National Police (CNP)

128 Index

cocaine 8, 10, 11, 20, 26, 32, 33, 34, 74, 121;
    see also Operation Beanpot
Colima Cartel 10
Colombia 74, 78; Cali Cartel 25, 26, 29, 34, 83;
    Medellin Cartel 25–26, 29; *see also* Operation
    Beanpot
Colombian National Police (CNP) 83–85, 89
common purpose 97
Connolly, John 31–32, 63, 64–66, 67–68, 97
constitutional law, United States 76, 89–90, 91
contraband sales 1, 2, 5, 17, 30–31, 39, 40, 41, 73,
    74, 99, 100; *see also* drug trafficking
Convention Against Organized Crime 1, 79
Corona, Felipe de Jesus 11
Coronel Villarreal, Ignacio "Nacho" 9, 10
corruption 2, 5; capture of governmental institutions
    18, 21; Colombia 34, 83; detectable traces of 31–32,
    34; of FBI in Bulger case 31–32, 62, 65, 66, 97; of
    local law enforcement 44, 58; prosecutions and 41
Cosa Nostra, La (LCN) 7, 38, 43, 44, 46–47, 57, 58, 59,
    60–61, 62, 63, 64, 71, 73
counter-terrorism 25–26, 27, 123
covert investigations 42, 45, 48–53, 56–57
criminal forfeiture of proceeds of crime 46
criminal punishment 39
CTRs *see* currency transaction reports (CTRs)
Curaçao 90
currency transaction reports (CTRs) 103, 109, 110
customary international law 75–76, 77, 85–86

DAS *see* Administrative Department of Security (DAS),
    Colombia
data thefts 116, 117
Davis, Debbie 66, 68
de la Madrid Hurtado, Miguel 8
DEA *see* Drug Enforcement Administration (DEA),
    United States
Department of Homeland Security, United States 91
Department of Justice, United States 58, 83, 89
detectable traces of organized crime 30–36; activities
    and capacities 30–31, 40–41; books and records 34,
    122–123; corruption and intimidation 31–32, 34;
    encryption and 122–123; killings and capacity for
    warfare 32–33; patterns of routine operations 35–36;
    transnational operations 32
disruptive innovation 122
distribution, Sinaloa Cartel 10–11, 20
drones 123
Drug Enforcement Administration (DEA), United
    States 8, 12, 25, 61, 79, 81; *see also* Operation
    Beanpot
drug trafficking 8, 34, 46; drones 123; Internet and
    116; Mexico 7–14, 20, 33; new products 116, 121;
    reducing drug sales 20, 74; *see also* Operation Beanpot

effects principle 85–86
"El Chapo" *see* Guzmán Loera, Joaquín "El Chapo"
electronic crime *see* Internet crime
electronic surveillance 28, 31, 37, 42, 44, 45, 58–59,
    64; new forms of 123; Operation Beanpot 83–85,
    86–87, 90–91
El-Hage case 76
encryption 122–123
enforcement costs 18, 21
Escobar, Pablo 6, 25–26, 28, 78, 83
European arrest warrant 78
European Union 78
Europol 79
evidence 41, 42, 44, 49, 78, 95, 118–119
extortion 1, 2, 5, 17, 20, 21, 30–31; labor racketeering
    46; new technology and 116, 121
extradition: in Operation Beanpot 88–90, 91; of Pablo
    Escobar 25
extradition treaties 77–78, 88–89, 91, 95–96
extraterritorial statutes 75–76

Facebook 123
FATF *see* Financial Action Task Force (FATF)
Federal Bureau of Investigation (FBI) 27, 44–45, 52,
    56, 58, 60–61; attaché relationships 79; Bulger case
    31–32, 62–68, 97
Federal Court of Appeals for the Second Circuit 76
Félix Gallardo, Miguel Ángel 8, 9
Fifth Amendment rights 76
finances of organized crime: books and records 34,
    104–105, 122–123; *see also* money laundering
Financial Action Task Force (FATF) 104, 109, 111
Financial Crimes Enforcement Network (FinCEN)
    108, 109, 110, 111, 112
Flemmi, Stephen 61–62, 63, 64–67, 68
Foley, Tom 60, 61, 62, 63, 64
Foreign Intelligence Surveillance Act Amendments
    (2008) 76
Foreign Narcotics Kingpin Designation Act 12
forfeiture of proceeds of crime 46
Fourth Amendment rights 76, 91
France 27, 78
future of organized crime 121–124; drones 123;
    encryption 122–123; new alliances 122; new
    products 116, 121–122; technological changes
    122–123; virtual currencies 107, 111, 112, 122;
    see also Internet crime

gambling 1–2, 46; new technology and 116, 122
Germany 78
Glenny, Misha 7
globalization *see* transnational organized crime
Gon, Zhenli Ye 10, 12
Gonzalez, Albert 117

Gonzalez, Alberto 82
Google 123
Great Britain 26–27
Greig, Catherine 68
Grella, John 82, 83, 87, 88, 91
Guadalajara Cartel 8–9, 10
Guantanamo Bay, Cuba 90
Gulf Cartel 9, 33, 34
Guzmán Loera, Joaquín "El Chapo" 8, 9, 10–11, 12–14, 28

Hafer, Zachary 82, 83–86, 87, 88, 89, 90–91
Halloran, Brian 66
Hamadei case 78
heroin 8, 10, 116, 121
Hoffa, Jimmy 41
horse race-fixing operations 32, 61–62, 64

import-export companies 105
informal value transfer services (IVTS) 106
informants 42, 45, 51, 53–54, 57, 58–59, 60; Bulger case 31–32, 62–68; Operation Beanpot 81–82
intelligence agencies 6, 7, 24, 27, 28
international law 32; constraints of 74–76, 85–86; effects principle 85–86; of human rights 26–27
international law enforcement cooperation 77–80, 94–97; attaché relationships 79, 88, 89; common purpose 97; effects principle 85–86; European arrest warrant 78; extradition treaties 77–78, 88–89, 91, 95–96; Internet crime 119–120; multi-state conventions 79; Mutual Legal Assistance Treaties (MLATs) 77, 79, 95–96; shared credit 97; trust 97; *see also* Operation Beanpot
International Monetary Fund 111
Internet crime 115–120; data thefts 116, 117; encryption 122–123; evidence collection problems 118–119; limits of international cooperation 119–120; new criminal businesses 116, 121–122; obstacles to investigations of 116–118; virtual alliances 122
intimidation 2, 5, 17–18; detectable traces of 31–32; new measures against 45, 56
Iraq War 22
Irish gang wars, Boston 57, 59–60
Israel 27
Italian mafia 29, 31–32, 46–47, 57, 58, 59, 60–61, 62, 64
IVTS *see* informal value transfer services (IVTS)

Juárez, Mexico 24, 28, 33
Juárez Cartel 9, 33

Kefauver, Estes 44, 58
Kefauver Committee 58
Kelley, Clarence M. 60

Kennedy, Robert 44, 45, 58, 69
Killeen, Donald 59
Killeens 59–60
killings, as detectable traces of organized crime 32–33
Kleiman, Mark 20
"Know Your Customer" rules 109
Kroger, John 46–47

labor racketeering 46
law enforcement and organized crime 5, 7, 27–28, 37–55; big data use 123; Bulger case 28–29, 31–32, 56–69, 97; charging strategies 54–55; criminal punishment 39; investigative difficulties 40–42, 43–44, 58; money laundering statutes 37, 46, 103, 108–109, 110–111; motivation of law enforcement 80; new investigative techniques 45, 48–55, 56–57, 58–59; new organizational structures 44–45, 56–57, 58; new strategies for prosecutors 48–55; new substantive statutes 37, 46, 56–57, 59; prosecution difficulties 41, 45, 58; reallocating responsibilities 44–45; responses to encryption 122–123; responses to intimidation 45, 56; witness protection programs 45, 56, 59, 60; *see also* international law enforcement cooperation
law of war 25–26
LCN *see* La Cosa Nostra (LCN)
Lehr, Dick 63, 64
letters rogatory 79
loan-sharking 1–2, 46, 60, 61
Los Alamos Laboratory 52

Malaga (ship) 86–88
marijuana 8, 10, 11, 13, 20, 74, 121
Martorano, John 67, 68
Mattioli, Dave 62
Medellin Cartel 6, 25–26, 29, 34
Merino-Cuaran, Bernardo Alberto *85*
methamphetamine 10
Mexico 19, 26, 28, 74, 79, 107; bulk cash smuggling 101–102; Juárez 24, 28, 33; Sinaloa Cartel 7–14, 20, 33, 34; Zeta Cartel 29, 33, 34
military 6, 7, 18, 19, 25, 27, 28, 34, 74, 124
Miranda rights 76
MLATs *see* Mutual Legal Assistance Treaties (MLATs)
money laundering 31, 99–112; bulk cash smuggling 101–102, 111–112, 123; business fronts 103–104; criminal statutes 37, 46, 103, 108–109, 110–111; currency transaction reports (CTRs) 103, 109, 110; informal value transfer services (IVTS) 106; international standards for combating 109; "Know Your Customer" rules 109; Operation Beanpot 81–82; reasons for failure of regulation 111–112; regulatory regime 37, 46, 102, 108–112; scale of 111; Sinaloa Cartel 11–12; structured deposits 102–103;

130 Index

suspicious activity reports (SARs) 109, 110, 111, 112; trade-based laundering 105–106; using other groups' laundering systems 106–107; virtual currencies 107, 111, 112
Morcillo-Molina, May Adolfo *85*
Morris, John 65–66, 67
Mossack Fonseca 104
Mullens 59, 60
multi-state conventions 79
Mutual Legal Assistance Treaties (MLATs) 77, 79, 95–96

National Drug Intelligence Center 101
National Security Agency (NSA) 27
National Security Council, United States 3, 5, 21–22, 31, 32
national security threat concept 21–22
Netherlands 90
New York 21, 44, 56, 60
New York Times 13
Nieto, Enrique Pena 14, 18

Office of Foreign Assets Control, United States 9
Office of the United States Marshals 45
offshore tax havens 104
Omnibus Crime Control and Safe Streets Act (1968) 59
O'Neill, Gerard 63, 64
Operation Beanpot 81–92, *84*, *85*, 94, 96, 97; effects principle 85–86; following smuggling activities 86–88; indictment and extradition 88–90, 91; money laundering 81–82; prosecution 90–92; Romania 87–88, 97; wiretapping 83–85, 86–87, 90–91
opioids 116, 121
Orejuelai, Miguel Rodriguez 34
organized crime: business strategies of 35–36; characteristics of 5, 7; definitions of 1–3; major businesses of 1–2, 5, 17; seriousness of threat 21–23; structure and finances 34; *see also* detectable traces of organized crime; future of organized crime; law enforcement and organized crime; money laundering; state strategies for addressing organized crime; transnational organized crime
organized crime strike forces 45, 58
O'Sullivan, Jeremiah 61, 64–65, 67, 68
overt investigations 42, 48, 52, 53
Oxycontin 116

Palma Salazar, Héctor Luis "El Güero" 9
PAWs *see* provisional arrest warrants (PAWs)
"Pizza Connection" case 103
Posadas Ocampo, Juan Jesús 9
Posse Comitatus Act (1878) 27
prestige, rewards of 57
prior conspiracy law 46

privacy laws 104
provisional arrest warrants (PAWs) 88–89
public fear of organized crime 2, 18
public trust in government 2–3, 18

race-fixing operations 32, 61–62, 64
Racketeer Influenced and Corrupt Organizations Act (1970, RICO) 37, 46, 56, 59, 60, 67, 68, 77
Ramirez, Noe 12
Regon Aguilar, Jesus Enrique 34
remittances 106
Rempel, William 34
Reynosa Gonzalez, Jose 11
RICO *see* Racketeer Influenced and Corrupt Organizations Act (1970, RICO)
robberies, detectable traces of 40–41
Romania 87–88, 97
Ruales-Vallejo, Fidel Alberto *85*
Rule of Specialty 78, 91
Russian mafia 107

Salcedo, Jorge 34
Salemme, Frank 66–67
Sarhatt, Lawrence 65
SARs *see* suspicious activity reports (SARs)
Security and Exchange Commission 117
shared credit 97
shell corporations 82, 104, 105
Sinaloa Cartel 7–14, 20, 33, 34
smuggling: bulk cash 101–102, 111–112, 123; drones 123; Operation Beanpot 86–88; Sinaloa Cartel 10–11
smurfing 103
state strategies for addressing organized crime 5–6, 7, 17–23, 24–29; alliances 6, 28; choosing a system of rules 25–26; choosing instruments of state force 27–28; elimination of organizations 18–19; major concerns 17–18; reducing capabilities of organized crime 19; reducing most dangerous harms 19, 20–21; seriousness of threat 21–23; transnational organized crime 73–74; *see also* international law enforcement cooperation; law enforcement and organized crime
statutes 37, 46, 56–57, 59; extraterritorial 75–76; money laundering 37, 46, 103, 108–109, 110–111
Stern, Donald 66
structure of organized crime groups 34
structured deposits 102–103
Supreme Court, Colombia 25–26
Supreme Court, Israel 27
Supreme Court, United States 45, 91
surveillance 31, 42, 45, 58–59; new forms of 123; *see also* wiretapping
suspicious activity reports (SARs) 109, 110, 111, 112
"SWAT" capacity 28

tax havens 104
technology 122–123; big data 123; drones 123; encryption 122–123; new criminal businesses 116, 121–122; new forms of surveillance 123; virtual currencies 107, 111, 112, 122; *see also* Internet crime
terrorism 1, 2, 22, 25–26, 27, 123
terrorist groups 122
Tia Anita foods 11
Tijuana Cartel 9
trade-based money laundering 105–106
transnational organized crime 71, 73–80; constraints of international law and 74–76, 85–86; detectable traces of 32; state strategies for addressing 73–74; United States constitutional law requirements and 76, 89–90, 91; *see also* international law enforcement cooperation; Internet crime
Treasury Department, United States 109
treaties 75, 77–79, 95–96
trust: international law enforcement cooperation 97; public trust in government 2–3, 18
tunnel systems, Sinaloa Cartel 11, 12

undercover operations 31, 42, 45, 51, 83
United Nations Convention Against Organized Crime 1
United Nations Office on Drugs and Crime 111

United Self-Defense Forces of Colombia (AUC) 89
United States constitutional law 76, 89–90, 91
United States Marshals Service 45, 90
Uribe, Alvaro 89

Valachi, Joseph 58
vending machine company 66
violence: detectable traces of 32–33; as major state concern 17–18; reducing 20–21
virtual currencies 107, 111, 112, 122

war, law of 25–26
Weeks, Kevin 67, 68
WikiLeaks 117
Winter, Howie 59, 60, 61–62
Winter Hill Gang 29, 59, 60, 61–62, 64, 97
wiretapping 45, 58, 59; Operation Beanpot 83–85, 86–87, 90–91
witness protection programs 37, 45, 56, 58, 59, 60, 96
Wolf, Mark 67–68, 69, 91
Wyshak, Fred 62, 66–67, 68

Zambada García, Ismael "El Mayo" 9, 12
Zapata-Sanchez, Luis Alberto *85*, 89, 90
Zeta Cartel 29, 33, 34

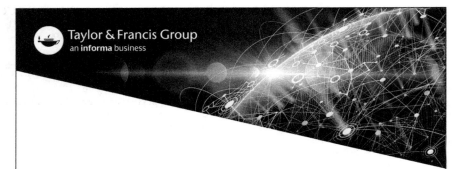

Taylor & Francis eBooks

www.taylorfrancis.com

A single destination for eBooks from Taylor & Francis with increased functionality and an improved user experience to meet the needs of our customers.

90,000+ eBooks of award-winning academic content in Humanities, Social Science, Science, Technology, Engineering, and Medical written by a global network of editors and authors.

TAYLOR & FRANCIS EBOOKS OFFERS:

- A streamlined experience for our library customers
- A single point of discovery for all of our eBook content
- Improved search and discovery of content at both book and chapter level

REQUEST A FREE TRIAL
support@taylorfrancis.com

PGSTL 07/18/2018